D1479070

# CHILDREN
# OF THE
# CONESTOGA

by
Clayton H. Gehman

THE BRETHREN PRESS

ELGIN, ILL.

**CHILDREN OF THE CONESTOGA**

Printed in the United States of America

Library of Congress Cataloging in Publication Data:

Gehman, Clayton H., 1909-
  Children of the Conestoga.

  1. Gehman, Clayton H., 1909- 2. Church of the Brethren—Clergy—
Biography. 3. Clergy—Pennsylvania—Conestoga Valley—Biography. 4.
Pennsylvania Germans—Biography. 5. Conestoga Valley, Pa.—Biogra-
phy. I. Title.
BX7843.G43A33      286'.5 [B]      78-7255
ISBN 0-87178-133-6

Published by the Brethren Press, Elgin, Ill.

Distributed by Two Continents Publishing Group,
30 E 42 St., New York, N.Y. 10017

# LOVE TO LIVE

*God is love.*
*Love is a human face reflecting the face of God.*
   *It is eyes shining with the happiness of heaven.*
   *It is a mouth smiling true affection without a trace of*
     *seduction.*
   *It is a tongue saying, "I love you," and leaving you as free*
     *and bright*
        *as the early spring robin.*
*It is a kiss creating neither claim nor regret.*
*It is a caress without a sense of clutching.*

*Love is the creative power of God at work where people*
   *need each other.*

*Love is the blessed Jesus still going about, doing good and*
   *saying,*
     *"Come unto me all you who labor and are*
     *heavy laden,*
     *and I will give you rest."*

*Love is a person in whom God dwells.*

*God is love.*

# CONTENTS

# INTRODUCTION

This "little book," as Clayton Hurst Gehman calls it, deserves to be read thoughtfully. It reveals the roots of a quiet person who is inwardly excited, outwardly enthusiastic, loving, and caring.

As a student in college and seminary Clayton H. Gehman secured a solid background in Bible and theology. Being a careful observer of persons and also concerned about them, he became a disciplined student of psychology and received a graduate degree in this field.

His roots, his scholarly pursuits, together with his love of people enable him to relate to persons in a positive and helpful way. Many call him Pastor Gehman because they know him as an understanding counselor, an effective preacher and teacher. For forty-four years Clayton H. Gehman served as a pastor of churches in Illinois, Maryland, and Pennsylvania. He has always been active in the areas in which he served and gives eager support to the larger ministry of the church of Jesus Christ. For a while he served as a hospital chaplain; he continues during retirement to serve in a local hospital.

Read carefully the poem with which this volume is introduced. *Love to Live* reveals the faith of Clayton H. Gehman. This faith enables him to sense the movement of the Spirit in his own children and grandchildren, in the "children of the Conestoga," and in all of God's children.

*Stewart B. Kauffman*
*Elgin, Illinois*

# PROLOGUE

Love lives!

In this family narrative I shall try to relate what I have felt of living affection as one may sense it in the daily routine of life. I am writing this for my children and grandchildren, for my brothers and sisters and their children and grandchildren, and for all who may wish to take the time to read this story. The story is true. The details in a few cases are combinations of several events. Not all the items are in exact chronological order, but the content is authentic.

My life has been spent searching for the good, beautiful, and rational in the universe. I searched for decency and love in human beings and found both in abundant measure. I looked for the durable in that which passes away and found much that survives among the ruins of life. I looked for peace in the midst of strife and found the quiet assurance that the Creator knows his way around in the universe of which I am a living part. I reached for love in daily life and found God's resource in Jesus all sufficient. This is a word of happiness and appreciation expressed for the family and the community that gave me birth, life, and meaning.

## THE DAWNING

I was born into a family of love!

In the thin shade of a row of tall poplar trees that stood at the edge of the lawn in front of our house, I came to an awareness of my surroundings and my own separate selfhood. That dawning to beauty, love, and life still fills me with a sense of mystery. I want to trace those golden shafts of memory that flood my inner life with reflections of joy and appreciation.

Those tall poplar trees are the objects of my earliest recollections. I observed the trees, the leaves, and the moving clouds in the sky that day. I heard the sound of the leaves as the warm wind played around them. I saw them sway lazily in the breeze. I grasped the leaves that fell on me, held them, turned them, and called for my mother in great excitement. She came to my side. My sister Susie came too. Susie sat down on a pile of warm, dry leaves which my brother Eli had just raked together. Mom helped me to walk into my sister's outstretched arms.

Eli joined our group. He was holding a bird in his hand. A string was hanging from the bird's leg. I tried to walk to his side, but the bird squawked and flapped its wings toward me. Eli jerked the cord and pulled it back. The angry blackbird turned and sank its sharp bill into my brother's hand. He dropped the string, and the bird flew away with the twine hanging on its leg.

Blood began to trickle from Eli's hand. Mom hurried him into the house. Susie dropped me into the playpen and followed them immediately. The sudden change of mood bewildered me, and I cried. In moments Susie returned, and we sat together in contentment and love and played among the dry leaves in the warm sunlight.

Birds in large flocks gathered in the skies. Circling over the tops of the trees, their noisy excitement drowned out all other sounds. Descending on the branches of those straight and stately guardians of our lawn, the birds sang and swayed in the gentle breeze that stirred among those tall trees, until some sound or instinct gave signal for their departure. Then, in one black cloud, they rose high into the air and flew away beyond the mill.

Mom and Eli reappeared. Mom sat down with us on the pile of leaves. Eli showed me the neat, white bandage Mom had placed on his hand to cover the gash the bird had torn into his skin. Then he walked to the upper end of the yard and resumed his task of raking the leaves and carrying them out into the barnyard where he dumped them on the manure pile.

## AROUND THE KITCHEN STOVE

Our house was built against a hillside. The front side faced the mill. The first floor contained the big kitchen-dining room and the cellar back in the hillside. From the kitchen windows we could see upstream and downstream, the huge covered bridge with its heavy planks that rumbled like thunder when vehicles crossed over it rapidly, the dam, the trunk that channelled the water into the turbine, and the mill standing in the center of our view. The massive, stone structure of the mill, covered with a soft, yellowish sandy plaster was a glorious sight that my young mind embellished with heavenly grandeur.

The cellar was directly to the rear of the kitchen. In the far corner to the right going in, concrete walls surrounded a bubbling spring of water which supplied all our needs for water and refrigeration as well. Visitors always wanted to have a drink directly from that sparkling spring.

The second floor contained spacious living rooms and a bedroom. A third floor provided bedrooms for the family and all our employees. An attic was the fourth floor. Our house was full of people, workers and visitors. Sickness, such as the mumps, measles, chicken pox, and colds, sometimes made our house seem like a hospital, but mostly it was a house full of fun. There was worship and singing with my mother's accordion music. There was Bible reading in German and silent prayer.

Our family was large. At meals I sat in a highchair at Pop's left arm. Mom was on the opposite side of the table at his right arm. On Mom's side my sisters and our maids sat together. At the far end of the table all our mill employees sat, and from the lower end on my side, in order of their age, all my brothers sat. Sometimes, depending upon the work at the mill, twenty or more people ate at our table three times a day. On some occasions Grandma Susanna Sensenig Gehman was present. She was seventy-five-years-old and a widow. Pop's father had died long before I was born.

The kitchen stove was the place where our family gathered for evening fireside chats, serious conversations, and bedtime stories. During my awakening years at the Spring Grove mill, I was the youngest one in the family—the twelfth. Weaver, the first in our family, died before he was a year old. Henry was second and Jacob third. They were grown by the time I sat in the family circle. Samuel was fourth; Noah, fifth; and Isaac, sixth. Henry was married and living in his own home. Jacob was the teamster for Pop, and Samuel, Noah, and Isaac were Pop's main mill hands. Edwin and Eli were seventh and eighth. Susie and Katie, the only girls, were ninth and tenth. Phares was the eleventh, but he died in infancy. Katie was well in her fourth year by the time I was born.

In that family circle around the kitchen stove our maids entertained us with many strange and ghostly stories for evening fun and laughter. One story was about a man who had hidden lots of gold in his house. He spent much time counting his money and looking at his gold. Then, one day, in a great accident, his right arm was torn off at the elbow. When it was all healed, he asked a very good mechanic to make a golden arm for him. From then on the miser wore his gold on his arm. Unfortunately, the miser got sick and died. The mechanic and the undertaker were the only ones who knew about the golden arm.

Weeks after the burial, the mechanic became so obsessed with the idea of recovering the golden arm that he couldn't eat or sleep any more. One dark night he dug into the grave and got it. Later that night his bedroom was filled with a strange, eerie light. Frightening sounds echoed from wall to wall. A voice said, "Where is my golden arm?" The house shook; the windows rattled; the shingles on the roof clattered; and a voice boomed into the man's ears, "You've got it!" The man was so frightened he threw the golden arm from his bedroom window into the garden below. According to the story, he never saw the golden arm again. The maid impressed upon us that ill-gotten gold never permitted anyone to sleep in peace.

Susie enjoyed telling a story about her doll and Bart Horst, our nearest neighbor. The family laughed about it many times. The day after I was born, Susie and Katie took their dolls to play with the Bart Horst girls and to tell them the good news. Susie's doll had a small hole in its head, but she tried to keep it covered with the doll's hair.

"Another boy?" Mrs. Horst repeated in dismay. "It should have been a girl. Your mother has too many boys already."

"Oh, well," Susie said in the same downcast mood, "it's just good that it was something."

The Horst family laughed heartily.

"Well, anyway," Bart said, "that needs a celebration. Let me give your doll a drink." With that he proceeded to pour water into the hole in Susie's doll's head. "Now, your doll took a drink in honor of your new baby brother." He looked at Susie with a broad grin. "Be sure to tell your Mom about our celebration."

When Susie and Katie returned home that morning they were upset, and Susie declared, "If Bart Horst ever gets a hole in his head, I'll fill it with water!"

* * *

Jacob's right hand was crippled. The first and second fingers were gone—just little stubs. They were smashed in the horsepower gears when he was a small boy. The horsepower stood behind the barn. Four horses in teams of two were hitched to it at opposite ends of a long beam. At the center the beam was attached to gears and a shaft which transmitted power to a pulley near the barn. When the machine was in use, the four horses were driven in a circle around the central shaft. The pulley near the barn provided power to run a variety of machines that were used for grinding corn, shredding fodder, threshing wheat, shelling corn, and the like. It was not a plaything.

One evening when Pop went to a nearby sale, Henry, Jacob, and Samuel began to play "threshing machine" with the horsepower. One boy at each end of the long beams and one at the central gears provided the horses and the crew. The horsepower went round and round. The gears unrelentingly meshed their powerful teeth. A heap of straw provided the material for threshing. Each got his turn at the gears. Jacob, as the thresherman, placed his nandful of straw too close to the gears, and the teeth caught his fingers, smashing them. He screamed. Henry and Samuel reversed their action. But Jacob's fingers were a bloddy mass.

What should be done? Mom looked at the three frightened boys and Jacob's bloody hand. The maid ran to the neighbors for help. Someone got word to the family doctor —Doctor McConnell of Terre Hill. He stopped the bleeding. Then he called two surgeons to remove the fingers. When Pop came home, he found the surgeons completing their work. Jacob was sleeping, and the two fingers from his right hand were gone.

By the time I sat in those family circles Jacob was the main teamster for Pop's business. He faced all kinds of

7

weather conditions in summer and winter to make deliveries of flour to nearby and distant stores. One time in a blinding snow storm he was taking a bobsled load of flour in twelve-pound paper sacks to a big store in Reading. The sled struck an object that upset it. All the sacks were dumped into the deep snow. The horses broke loose—three of them, two hitched to the sled and one in front as the leader—and ran off into the blizzard. The lead horse, however, responded to Jacob's calling and returned. Jacob mounted him and rode as hard as the horse would go to overtake the runaways. Miles down the road he came upon them. Another traveler had stopped them and calmed them down. When everything was together, Jacob found that only two sacks were broken, so he completed his trip to Reading.

* * *

Henry's story held a good lesson for us all. With Jacob, Samuel, and Noah, Henry had raided a good neighbor widow's cantalope patch. But the cantalopes were not ripe enough to eat, so they covered their tracks and hid the green cantalopes, feeling confident that they had not been observed by anyone. Later in the season, however, the good woman called Henry as he was walking near her house.

"Henry, come here a minute."

"Yes," he answered as he walked to her fence, looking as calm and innocent as could be.

"My cantalopes are ripe now."

Henry was speechless.

"The other Sunday when you boys were in the patch you found only green ones. Now they are ripe, sweet and juicy, ready to be eaten. Tell your brothers, and come and help yourselves."

Henry stood still, wide-eyed, open-mouthed, and blushing all over his face.

8

"It's all right, Henry, don't you worry about that. A long time ago I was young. I was not altogether perfect myself."

"We, we, we knew better," Henry finally managed to say. "We shouldn't have done it."

"We all do things, even as older persons, that we know we shouldn't."

"Well, I—I," Henry stammered, "I'll pay you for the ones we spoiled!"

"Oh, no," she refused, "but I do want you to have some of the ripe ones. You must help yourselves." Then she walked into the house, leaving Henry standing alone in his embarrassment, calling after her that he would like to pay for the ones he stole, but she only shook her head and waved his offers aside.

Henry never went back to get any of those ripe cantalopes. Neither did the others.

* * *

In the warmth of the kitchen stove I listened to those family stories. I listened to the talking and laughing when the work was done. Peace, love, and happiness cradled me to sleep.

# The Mill

My father was the owner and manager of the Spring
Grove Roller Mill, located on the bank of the Conestoga
Creek near Terre Hill, Lancaster County, Pennsylvania.
Other nearby towns were Blue Ball, Goodville, Martindale, and New Holland. Reading was some fifteen miles
northeast. Lancaster was about the same distance to the
southwest.

Pop enjoyed the mill. He was deeply interested in his
business relationships with the people in the community.
Our neighborhood was composed, for the most part, of German-speaking people: Mennonites, German Baptists
(Dunkers), Amish, Reformed, and Lutheran.

All the farmers in the community sold their wheat to my
father. Our mill manufactured flour and did much other
grinding for the cattle, chicken, and hog growers in our
area. At threshing time the farmers brought the grain to
the mill by the wagon loads. The coming and going created
endless activity all day long. Five or six teams, sometimes
more, waited in line. The horses, chafing at their bits,
swinging their heads and tails to keep the flies away, displayed an array of beautiful color: black, brown, white,
gray, roan, sorrel, chestnut, and other mixtures with the
glistening foam of sweat sparkling in the sun.

My father's mill was widely known for the fine flour that
came from its machinery. When the bins were filled, he

10

often took me with him to the top floor up five flights of stairs to see the wheat and oats heaped high in the bins. In the busy season the machinery ran day and night to meet the orders that came from New York, Philadelphia, and many other cities in the East. My older brothers and our employees worked around the clock in shifts. Deliveries to stores in local towns were made regularly by wagon. Extra teamsters were employed to help haul the flour to the East Earl Railroad Station for shipment to distant cities.

From my play corner in the mill office I became acquainted with our customers at a very early age. One evening, when all the machinery was running full-blast, Pop prepared to leave the office for the night. He closed the heavy door of the big safe in which he kept money and records of business transactions. Then he took me in his arms, locked the office door, and checked with all the workmen. As we started down the stairs to the ground-floor exit, four big, gaunt-looking black men confronted us. I was afraid and hid my face in my father's shoulder.

"Are you Sammy Gehman?"

"Yes." There was a trace of surprise in Pop's voice.

"Sammy," a gentle voice said, "I'm Ike Patterson from the Welsh Mountain Black People's Settlement."

I looked up. The men had stepped back to the ground floor.

"These men are my neighbor's," Ike said. "We heard that you might be willing to help us."

"How? In what way?"

"Food."

They all looked at my father with concern in their eyes.

"Our children are hungry, and we have nothing to give them. We can't get jobs. Black men are not wanted. Our crops up on the mountain are not yielding much." Ike spoke slowly and softly.

At my home we spoke the Low German language, com-

11

monly called "Pennsylvania Dutch." So the only part of the conversation I understood was the use of my father's name. However, I did understand Pop's response. He gave them each a large sack of flour and many small bags of cornmeal. But what I understood better still, later on, was the strong friendship that grew in our family with Ike Patterson. Pop gave him work at the mill, on the farm, and around the house. Ike regularly cleaned our barn stables and our privy. He cheerfully performed many chores no one else wanted to do. As time went on, Ike Patterson's love and confidence was expressed in much loftier ways in his association with my father.

Ike shared his problems as leader of a black community with my father. He spoke of his hope for the future of his people under freedom. He tried to encourage them to have faith in their own abilities and to accept greater responsibility for their own welfare. His conversation was descriptive of a great dream, a dream which in time was immortalized by another good and famous black man: Dr. Martin Luther King, Jr.

\* \* \*

The mill dam was always a great attraction. Neighborhood boys gathered there with my brothers. The spillway and the trunk channel were sufficiently dangerous to make the place exceedingly alluring. The trunk channel conducted the water from the dam, through the dam breast wall, into the turbine which provided power for the machinery of the mill. At the inlet a grate prevented driftwood and other refuse from flowing into the turbine. Several planks spanned the top of the wooden channel, mainly to provide a footbridge. The channel was deep and about six feet wide.

One day the neighborhood boys played a game there which involved a dash over the footbridge. The leader threw a stick over the channel and called out the names of two other players. The two called ran for the stick. The one who got it was the leader for the next round of the game. At one point Edwin and Eli, then eight and seven, were named to be the runners. They both ran as fast as they could go. A serious collision occurred at the footbridge. Eli lost his balance and fell into the trunk channel. He was unable to swim. The wooden walls, slippery and wet, provided no holds. The older boys tried to rescue him, but he was out of their reach. Frantic and spent, Eli sank under the water. Edwin summoned help. Samuel got to the spot first. He threw himself down flat on the planks and grasped Eli's body, which was still floating below the surface, and drew him out, blue, limp, and unconscious. Samuel used his best skill to revive him. Water flowed from Eli's mouth, nose, and ears as Samuel worked on him. In a few suspense-laden moments Eli began to breathe. Soon he regained consciousness as the breath of life came back into his body.

Pop put an end to that game. He took Eli into the house for a rest and dry clothing. Most significantly, Pop ordered his carpenters to cover the trunk completely. By the time I was old enough to play there, it was covered with ground and grass.

The dam breast, with its big spillway, stretched well over two hundred freet from the front to the rear of the mill. The huge, old water wheel still stood in its place inside the southeast corner of the mill. It was no longer in operation. The turbine provided more efficient water power, but it was still a great curiosity. At that corner the spillway wall began and stretched one hundred feet to the other side of the creek. It was "verboten" territory. The boys were not to play there because the danger was too great.

From the covered bridge below the spillway, one could see the enormity of the wall. Built with large sandstones, it stood fifteen feet high and over one hundred feet long. At the bottom wooden breakers were built into the wall to keep the falling water from wearing away the foundation. The logs were similar in appearance to railroad ties and projected outward about four feet with six inch spaces between them. Normally they were two or three inches under water. In the dry season, when the water was low, both the spillway and the breakers were exposed. Snakes, turtles, bloodsuckers, and numerous other little creatures of the creek crept around in the sun on top of the logs and the wall.

Though forbidden territory, the boys would often play there. It was too much to expect them not to be lured into that fascinating area, especially when the neighborhood group gathered and the spirit of adventure swelled in each young breast.

One day a very large bloodsucker was discovered, and all the boys pressed against each other to get a good look. At the moment when the pressure was greatest, Eli stepped on a loose stone on top of the spillway wall. The stone turned, and Eli fell down upon the breakers. Fortunately he managed to straddle one and hold on. But the incident created another tense moment for the community boys group. They formed a hand to hand chain along the side of the wall over the rocks and roots protruding from the steep bank and carried out an ingenious rescue. Eli was safe with a sore bottom and wet feet. They kept their secret well for many years.

## GRANDMA SUSANNA SENSENIG GEHMAN

My Grandfather Moses Gehman died at the age of sixty-seven on the second of May in 1890. But Grandma Susanna Sensenig Gehman lived to be eighty-one. She maintained a home of her own in Spring Grove. Henry, after his marriage, lived in one side of her house, and she depended upon him for help in many ways. Finally, because of illness, she was compelled to give up housekeeping. She spent the remainder of her life with us. Her presence in our home added a memorable dimension to my life.

In spite of her affliction, Grandma was still very active and courageous. She drove her own horse and buggy. My older brothers and sisters often rode with her when she visited her sister, our Aunt Lucy and her husband, Uncle Hen, on their farm located along the pike that led from Blue Ball to Ephrata. She had many other close friends on her visiting list, so to go driving with her was always regarded as a great treat. It meant loving companionship, a pleasant buggy ride, and visiting where cookies, lemonade, and homemade root beer were served. Sometimes quarrels arose over the question of whose turn it was to ride with her. Grandma would say, "Decide peacefully or none will ride with me today."

Grandma was the tallest person in our family, slender, trim, and well-dressed. She was beautiful! When my turn came to ride with her, I soon discovered a warm, cozy, confidence in her presence. She always seemed to understand my questions before I asked them. She made me feel that she felt the way I felt about things and people. She was my earliest intimate teacher. One time on a trip with her, I noticed a difference between the horse she drove—a grayish-brown mare named Pet—and the one Pop drove. Pop's favorite horse was a blueish-gray gelding named Prince. I asked a few elemental questions about shape and elimination processes.

"Pet is a mother horse," she answered immediately. "She is the mother of several big horses now working on Uncle Hen's farm. God made her that way so she could have baby horses."

Her answer was completely satisfactory to me. She simply and easily allayed my curiosity.

Grandma Gehman also gave me my earliest lessons in daily devotions. When illness kept her in bed, I spent many mornings with her as she read from her German Bible. I bowed my head and folded my arms when she did. I felt her mood of worship and understood her prayers. Always at the close of her prayers, she held me in her arms and said, "Gott liebt uns."

One day as I was playing in Grandma's bedroom, she was sewing and using safety pins to hold some of her materials together. Quietly, without being noticed, I picked up one of those pins and began to play with it. I went to the window overlooking the meadow and the mill dam so that Grandma would not see me. There I opened and closed the pin for a long time.

"What are you doing?" she asked me.

"Nothing," I replied, but I sensed that my silence caused her to feel concern. Suspecting that she might ask me to come to her bedside, I put the pin in my mouth. But she quietly continued with her sewing. The pin in my mouth was open. I moved it around with my tongue. I felt the sting

16

of the sharp point. The pin went back into my throat and my fun ended. Coughing, choking, and crying, I ran to Grandma's bedside. She was frightened.

"Liddy, Liddy," she called. "Hurry, come. Something is wrong with Clayton."

Mother's maiden name was Lydia Weaver Horst. At the age of sixteen, she married my father. She was a slender, little woman, never weighing much over a hundred pounds, but she was nimble, energetic, full of fun. She carried a living, breathing love in her heart that filled our whole house. Her calm, smiling, soft-blue eyes always took away every fear and assuaged every pain.

I heard her coming up the steps.

"Not too fast! Remember, Liddy!"

I did not know the reason for Grandma's word of caution. The sound of her approaching footsteps meant relief. Later I learned that this happy, little woman—whose own father, my Grandfather Jacob Horst, used to say, "When Liddy was a child she lived on the wind"—was carrying her thirteenth child in her womb.

I swallowed the safety pin.

"What must we do now?" Grandma asked.

"Get him to the doctor!" Mom sent word to Pop, and in a short time Prince was tied to the hitching post in front of Doctor McConnell's office.

"The pin seems to have gone down without causing any trouble," the doctor said. He rechecked my mouth and throat.

"What can we do?" Pop asked.

"I think if you feed the boy string beans, nothing but string beans, the pin might pass without any trouble. If you don't find the pin in two or three days, the boy will have to go to the hospital. It will have to be located and removed."

For a while, mealtimes and sitting on the potty got much attention. Everyone encouraged me to eat my string beans, but there was some fear that the remedy might not work. It did. Mom burst out in her characteristic shout of joy and laughter that always sent waves of delight through our house.

"The pin! Here it is!" she exclaimed.

\* \* \*

Grandma's illness did not destroy her artistic nature. Our house had a second floor sun porch which extended all the way across the front. A high banister with a closed latticework made it a safe place for older ones and children alike. I spent many days there with Mom and Grandma, watching the activities at the mill and along the creek as well as the farmers in their fields on the south side of the Conestoga Valley. From her place on that sun porch, Grandma painted a picture of the mill with a two-horse wagon loaded with corn standing on the ramp for unloading. A farmer is nearby scooping the corn into the hoist barrel. Grandma made the picture into patches and sewed them on a blanket. That applique work is still a prized possession in our family.

Grandma became very familiar with the routine at the mill. She knew which day of the week the various customers came to have their grinding done. If some unfamiliar wagon appeared or a regular customer did not, she asked about it at mealtime.

"What happened to Philip Schwenkfelder? I did not see his team at the mill today."

"The fifth-wheel of his wagon broke, and he spent the day at Spring Grove in Taylor's Blacksmith Shop. He'll come tomorrow."

"Who was that new man with that fine-looking team of gray mules?"

"That was Harry Beckerman. He just moved to Mike Horning's place last week."

18

"Wasn't this George Zimmerman's day to come?"

"One of his cows got sick. He stayed home to wait for the doctor."

"And John Hoover didn't come either."

"He attended the big sale in New Holland. He wants to buy more beef steers to put out on his pasture for the summer."

Pop always answered kindly because he was still her "Sammy." He knew that Grandma's main concern was "Is everything all right with Sammy."

Grandma was very patient in her affliction. One day as we sat quietly on the sun porch she said, "I'm waiting, just waiting."

"What are you waiting for, Grandma?"

She drew me up close to her side. I could feel her warm heart beating against my face. "I'm just waiting on the Lord," she said and drew me more tightly into her thin arms.

I had no idea that she was thinking about the nature of her illness and that, given time, it would take her life away. In her waiting, though, she was always alert, always watching. Hardly a movement escaped her keen eyes. One day a little, unnoticed fire was burning in the autumn grass near the bridge.

"You'd better go and tell Sammy."

I ran down to the mill. Many customers were standing in the office with my father. I crept under their coats to Pop's side. "Sammy," I said, "there's a fire burning in the grass near the bridge."

The men laughed. But Pop understood that a message for "Sammy" came from Grandma. He put his arm around me to reassure me.

The fire had quickly spread to a pile of dry boards under the bridge and to the wagon shed near the mill. With buckets, shovels, and brooms the men extinguished the flames

19

and agreed that it might have reached the bridge and the mill in a few more minutes.

* * *

A group of gypsies came to our mill. They asked Pop for permission to camp in the mill meadow for a week. He gave them the privilege to do so. From the sun porch we watched them at work and at play.

A happy group of people—plump, smiling, and brown—the gypsies were vigorous and muscular men whose women were friendly, shapely, and colorfully dressed. The children played along the creek bank and in the meadow. At dusk, from their campfire, came the sound of music, singing, and laughter. It rang all along the lovely, misty, meadow-land. In the mornings and evenings they engaged in basket-weaving. During the day they peddled them from house to house.

Some people in our community were afraid of them and said that Pop should not have allowed them to camp in our meadow. Some said gypsies hypnotized people and animals. They could lure children away from home. They could pick your pockets and steal your chickens in your presence and you wouldn't know it. A gypsy woman was supposed to be able to bewitch a man and take his money from him while he was in a trance. None of those fearful things happened. But many of our neighbors were glad to see the gypsies pack up their belongings and move away.

* * *

On her very best days and in good weather, Grandma would ask Pop to hitch Pet to her buggy for a drive to Aunt Lucy's place. One day on our way back home Pet stumbled and fell. She made no move to get up. Grandma went to Pet's head and took hold of the bridle to encourage her to get up, but she would not do it. In a little while a man came by. He tied his horse to a fence post and came to help us.

"Did she break a leg?"

"I don't know," Grandma said. "She just stumbled and fell."

"She might have twisted an ankle."

"I saw no obstacle in the road."

"Well," the man said, "Let's unhitch her and get the buggy away from her. Then we'll try and get her up." When the harness was unhooked and the buggy pulled away, he grasped Pet's bridle and jerked it forward and upward, urging Pet to get up. She groaned and pawed the road for a little while and got up. The man examined her completely.

"Is she all right?" Grandma asked.

"I see nothing wrong except that she is holding that back foot on the right a bit crooked." He pointed for Grandma to see. "Let's hitch her up again. She might just get you home without any more trouble." He hitched her to the buggy. "Everything seems to be all right as far as I can tell. I think you'll have a safe trip home."

"Thank you, I hope so too," Grandma said.

"Say, Ma'am, seems I ought to know that horse. You don't happen to be Sammy Gehman's mother, do you?"

"Yes, I am." There was a note of pride in Grandma's voice.

"Well, now, I'm just right glad I came along in time to help you. I'm Joe Blowder. Sammy's a good friend of mine."

"That's nice." Grandma was preparing to go.

"Who's that young fellow you got with you?"

"Oh, this is my grandson." She slapped the reins on Pet's back. Pet started at a brisk walk but she limped.

"Take care! You'll make it. Get that nice-looking boy home safely."

"I will." Grandma looked back and smiled; then she turned to me and said, "That was nice of him to say that, wasn't it?"

It was easy to see that Grandma was just as pleased as I was about Joe Blowder's remark.

Months later I was riding with Pop in the spring wagon loaded with flour for stores in New Holland. We met Joe Blowder. Pop stopped to talk to him.

"Du bist der Joe Blowder!" I shouted. Pop was surprised and told me to keep quiet.

"Thank you for helping my mother with Pet sometime back."

"Oh, it was just a little thing," Joe said. "How's the mare doing?"

"She's still lame. Getting old and bad on her legs, I guess."

When they were ready to go, Joe looked at me and smiled; Then he said to Pop, "That's a bright boy you got there."

Joe Blowder probably never knew how much those words meant to me. It was my first look at myself through the eyes of someone outside of our own family. Years later, when I was grappling with the problems of early adolescence, another person made a remark at our dinner table that fired my brain to lofty imaginations.

Changing plans were taking shape in our family. Pop often talked about putting a new house and barn on our eighty acres of land adjacent to the mill property. The work was begun. Ike Patterson worked for Pop as the building program proceeded. Pet was turned loose in the meadow that stretched westward from the mill, under the bridge, along the main stream of the Conestoga, to the lower end of our property where an old, abandoned lime-kiln stood against an abrupt hillside. There she would have freedom of movement and good grazing. In addition, it provided Grandma with a consoling pastime. From her chair on the sun porch, she could watch Pet walk around in the meadow.

I spent much time there with Grandma watching Pet, listening to the sound of the water rushing over the spillway, the humming of the machinery at the mill, the voices of men calling orders to one another about the new buildings that were already under construction, and to the autumn leaves rustling in the wind.

One night Pet died. The next morning Grandma sat in her chair in the warm sunlight. She didn't say a word, but her eyes constantly scanned the meadow. She seemed to be studying every feature of the old, unpainted, covered bridge; she watched the water in its pouring, churning torrent below the spillway; she looked across the creek to the little, white, stone house that stood along the road and partly hidden from our view by the bridge. Suddenly she seemed to become aware of my presence.

"Pet is gone," she said. "She was weary and old like I am. Maybe she died somewhere in the high grass. You go and tell Sammy that I can't see Pet anywhere."

At the mill office, Pop was so involved in his accounts that I could hardly get his attention.

"Pet is gone."

But he did not hear me. His pencil kept on writing.

"Pet is lost. Grandma is afraid that she is dead."

He still did not hear me.

"Sammy, Sammy," I called, "Pet is lost. She's gone!"

He laid his pencil down and looked at me. "Did Grandma send you down to tell that?"

I nodded.

"Well, we'd better take a look." He rose from his chair and walked to the office window overlooking the meadow. "I can't see her either," he said. Taking my hand, he said, "Yes, we must find Pet."

23

My father was a friendly, soft-spoken person of average height and weight. His high, squarish, balding forehead was well-formed. His full, smiling face had two distinctive features. One was his bright, deep-blue eyes. The other was the little specks of tobacco that usually clung to the corners of his mouth. Although he was slightly round shouldered and flat-chested, he always wore simple, clean, store-purchased clothes and carried himself with quiet but warm-hearted dignity.

"Let's find Ike," Pop said, and we left the office. Outside he made another effort to locate Pet. She was not in sight. We walked across the wide driveway and up the lane toward the barn where Ike was working.

He saw us coming and came to the door. "Trouble?"

"Pet is gone and Grandma is worried." Pop looked back toward the meadow. "Maybe you can find her?"

"Sure, we'll find her." Ike took my hand.

Ike was a big man. All in our family were little people beside him. His shoulders—broad, straight, and full-chested—gave the impression of great strength. His footprints in the soft barnyard ground were twice as large as my father's. His face was bright and black, and his white teeth flashed like pieces of glass in the sunlight when he talked or smiled.

Pop returned to the mill. Ike and I searched through the meadow, under the bridge, behind every pile of drift wood, and in the heavy undergrowth. We went over the area a second time. But we could not find Pet. Then Ike headed toward the deserted limekiln. We climbed the slope, making our way through the high grass and over the rocks to the top of the old furnace wall. The first pit was full of farm machinery junk. At the bottom of the second pit, which was still empty, we found Pet's dead body.

"There she is." Ike spoke with pity in his voice.

"Pet is dead." I could hardly believe it.

24

"Yeah, no more buggy rides with her." Ike took my hand. "Well, let's go back and tell Sammy."

Pop broke the news to Grandma. She bowed her head and said, "I expected it." Tears moved slowly down over the wrinkles at the side of her nose. "What are you going to do with her?"

"We could call Bart Horst to come and get her for his foxes and hounds."

"Pet, meat for animals that make a fox chase?" Grandma shook her head. "No, not that!"

"The scavenger would take her to the glue factory."

Grandma remained silent.

"We could bury her in the pit where she died."

"With all that junk?"

"Well, Pet's dead. She selected her own grave. Ike can cover the junk with ground that we are hauling from the basement digging at the new house. He can make that junky limekiln into a nice cemetery for Pet."

Grandma smiled. "It's silly for me to feel this way about Pet, but I loved her."

"Ike can start right now," Pop said.

When the hauling was done and Ike was raking the ground for grass seeding, the man who lived on the adjoining farm stopped to talk to us.

"All that cleaning just for an old dead horse?" He sounded sarcastic. "Junk cleared away, pits filled, ground leveled, grass planted." He laughed. "Flowers, I suppose, next spring."

Giving the man a glance, Ike said, "Well, this mare served Sammy's mother some twenty years, and she never caused anybody any trouble. If Sammy and his mother want her buried in this manner on their own land, why should you be troubled about it?" Ike stopped raking and looked at the visitor.

25

"It's none of my business. I meant nothing by it."

Ike smiled. "Then we'll keep right on changing this dump into a nice graveyard. We're doing this out of respect for Sammy's mother's fine sensitivities."

## THE NEW HOUSE AND BARN

There was constant action, people going back and forth day and night, between our big house at the mill and the new one up the road several hundred feet. As soon as the house was finished, we moved in, and early in April Harvey was born. Aunt Kate, Mom's sister, took me to her house at that time. Aunt Kate was older than Mom. Her children were grown and her husband, Uncle Davey, was sick. But she filled every day for the two months I was there with fun and laughter. Aunt Kate took me back home, just in time for me to watch the painters complete their work on our new house and barn.

Behind the barn, where the painters had been working all day, I found a bucket of red paint. It was nearly empty. With a stick I smeared the paint on my right leg from the knee to the foot. I hurried to show my mother the beautiful work I had done. She was aghast. Her face turned white.

"Why did you do that?" She stared in utter disbelief. "How will we ever get that paint off your leg?"

Frightened at her reaction, I tried to explain.

"If it makes the barn look nice, why doesn't it make my leg look nice?" I broke down in tears as Mom in alarm called for Pop.

"Boy, what in the world will you get into next?" He scolded as he applied the turpentine and thrust me into the porch pump trough. "Pump water on it," he said to Mom.

27

All went down the drain in a short time. "Don't do that again," he said sternly, "if you want to smear paint, put it on an old piece of board."

* * *

Mom had two brothers, Uncle Weaver and Uncle Noah, who were interested in Pop's plans. Uncle Weaver Horst moved his family into the big house at the mill as soon as we moved out. He bought the mill from Pop. Uncle Noah, who lived at the Conestoga Mill some miles down stream from Spring Grove, wanted our farm, but Pop would not sell it to him.

Luke, Uncle Weaver's youngest child, and I were closely attached cousins. We played together throughout the years of our childhood, sometimes at the dam in the shallow water, sometimes in our new, spacious lawn. Because of Luke's mother's illness, we were not allowed to play in her house. Even our activities outside often made her nervous. On one occasion Luke told me that his mother did not want him to play with me so much of the time.

"Why not?" I asked him.

"You are a common Dutch-farmer's child. My mother wants me to grow up to be an eloquent, English-speaking gentleman, not a vulgar farmer kid," he explained.

We were playing in our yard, running all the way around the house. In the laundry there was a box full of celery, fresh and ready for market. Each time we came around the house, we snatched a piece of celery. Pop, who caught us in the act, spanked me severely. Then he turned to Luke.

"Don't you touch me," Luke burst out. He faced my father firmly. "Don't you dare touch me with your Dutch-farmer hands. You are common, vulgar folks. We are refined, English-speaking people. Don't you touch me."

Pop was shocked. I can still see him stand and stare at Luke with his mouth open and his eyes wide.

My bottom burned.

Luke maintained his defiant posture.

When Pop's eyes and mouth returned to normal, he said, "No, I wouldn't lay a hand on you. You're not my son. But with all your English-speaking ability and refinement, you should have known better than to spoil my celery."

We stood in the brisk wind and bright sunlight of a frosty autumn morning—the three of us. My bottom was still hot from the whipping I had gotten. Pop and Luke faced each other at our front lawn gate. Neither one moved.

"I'm sorry I helped to spoil your celery," Luke said in a very dignified manner and with a calm voice. "I should have known better, even if Clayton did suggest it."

Pop looked at me with hard eyes.

I promised never to do it again.

Pop returned to the barn.

Luke opened the gate and went home.

*  *  *

The summer of 1912 was bewildering to me. Change had taken place very rapidly, and the work on the farm was varied and different: planting, harvesting, threshing, and all the other work was determined by the weather. Bad weather meant bad moods. I often felt alone. My sisters were busy in school and helping mother. Grandma's room was forbidden territory because of her sickness. One morning, on the sunny side of the big straw stack, I sat down and fell asleep. At dinner time Isaac awakened me.

"It's dinner time," he said. "Come in. Mom is worried about you."

I brushed the straw from my face and said, "You go and tell Mom I'm dead." Then I turned my face into the straw. But Isaac saw to it that I got to the house for dinner.

* * *

The John Hoover family lived directly across the road from our new home. The youngest child in their large family was my age. We often played together. One day he fell under large wagon wheels out in their field and was killed. The sadness that lay on our community following the accident added to my loneliness and bewilderment. In addition, Harvey, our new baby, took so much of my Mom's time that she had very little for me.

"You are a big boy now," she would explain. "Harvey is the baby, and we must take care of him. You can help with the work." Sometimes that made me feel proud. At other times I just felt like pushing Harvey off her lap.

The Bart Horst's were an interesting family and good friends. My sisters still played there much of the time, when they were not busy at home. Their house was down the road from ours and across the road. In the days of slavery, it had provided room at one end for all the slaves on the big farm. This large building stood on the edge of the slope that led down to the creek on the west side of the bridge. The whole hillside was woodland and filled with thick undergrowth. Their land extended far down along the woods that bordered the Conestoga. Tall horse-chestnut trees stood in their front lawn. Behind the house, in the woods, a large pack of hounds was kept in a shed. In a den under the tobacco shed, Bart kept the foxes he had captured for his fox chases. They stayed back in the dark corners of the den and appeared only at feeding time.

On a late November day Bart's place was the center of excitement in our community. It was the day of the fox chase. A huckster table was set up near the barn. Coffee, candy, tea, sandwiches, peanuts, and various kinds of pretzels were on sale. The air was chilly, and a light snow had fallen during the night. Several fires were burning near the huckster's table. Here observers and participants huddled in groups to warm themselves. The wooded slope toward the creek was sparkling in the sun.

From our living room we could see the crowd milling about between Bart Horst's big house and barn. We regarded the fox chase as a worldly pleasure, but it was so fascinating that even Mom and Pop spent some time watching the activities. The horsemen arrived, one after another, in pride and splendor. Horses were puffing out their frosty breath and pawing and prancing impatiently. Now and then one would rear upright in his eagerness to get into the chase. Some riders dismounted in order to keep their animals under control. One man jumped away from his horse as it reared up and fell over backward.

When Bart Horst brought the fox out of the den and exposed it to the hounds, a furor of howling and yelping arose. As Bart took the fox out into the field and released it, the dogs barked in a wild frenzy. The horses wheeled, pawed, reared, and pulled at the bridle reins. The riders sat alert and tense. Then the hounds were set free to take up the trail. The riders spread out along the various roads in the community as the hounds chased the fox around through the fields and thick undergrowth in the woods. No one ever knew which way the fox would turn. It was a frantic, wild dashing, in and out, back and forth through the fields, into the woods, and along the roads until at last the fox was cornered and captured. Then all the streaking colors of hounds, horses, riders, and fox came to a puffing, panting standstill in Bart Horst's barnyard. The chase was over.

In our view it was a sinful, worldly sport. We were not supposed to watch it, but we could not keep our eyes away. The immeasurable excitement and enjoyment all the participants seemed to experience was baffling to us. We explained it in the context of the wicked and sinful pleasures of this world.

Down at the mill my Uncle Weaver Horst was demonstrating a similar kind of yielding to worldliness. He used automobiles and trucks instead of horses and wagons. He installed telephones and other appliances as they became available. The old wagon shed that stood between the mill and the bridge was transformed into a garage and filled with trucks, cars, oil barrels, and gasoline tanks. The engines exhaled fumes that burned our noses and throats, causing us to choke and cough. How different from the horses, harnesses, and stables!

Uncle Weaver and his family said that our way was old-fashioned and out of date. Cars and trucks were more efficient, much more convenient, and less dangerous. They proved it by reminding us of the many accidents Jacob and Noah had with our horses. Horses were not always controllable!

One day Noah and Prince had some serious trouble. Coming from town in the spring wagon, they encountered a herd of steers crossing the road in front of them. Prince balked. Noah used the whip on him to make him go through the bellowing herd. Two of the steers charged Prince and swished him in the face with their tails. That was too much. The horse broke into a dead run with the wagon bouncing so severely that Noah fell from the seat back into the wagon bed. Prince went headlong for home. Pop heard the clatter coming over the bridge and saw what was happening. In a strong voice he called to Prince. The horse and wagon slid to a halt in front of the mill at the edge of the dam. Noah was still clinging to the bottom of the wagon bed.

Still, we held to our belief that horses were safer than automobiles, and we were on the lookout for evidence to prove our view. After a thunderstorm on a late Sunday afternoon, we were driving in our carriage along the road from Terre Hill to Martindale. An automobile without a top came toward us at a nice speed. Prince did not seem to mind the strange, chugging sound of the approaching car. We turned to our side and the automobile driver turned to his. But his front wheel slid into the soft, muddy berm of the road. His engine sputtered and stalled. He was stuck in the muddy ditch. The women, in their fancy garments, were splashed with the dirty water that was still rushing along in the gutter. They cried and clung to each other and to the upper side of the car to keep from falling into the yellow torrent.

Prince stood still. I held the reins. Pop went across the road and helped the people out of their vehicle. Then he walked to a nearby farm for help. The farmer came with a team of horses and pulled the motorcar out of the ditch. All the while the women were denouncing the fearsome buggy in which they had been riding. One declared that she would never again get into such a dangerous wagon. The driver brushed the mud from his gloves, persuaded the women to get into the machine, and went on his way.

Our controversy with Uncle Weaver and his family was deeper than horses, wagons, and motorcars. It was a matter of which church group was the right one to follow: the Old Orders or the new group. We favored the old. Uncle Weaver and his family supported the new. The conservative element urged the use of the German language in all services, denounced public-school education beyond fourth grade, favored excommunicating all who used telephones, electric appliances, motorized vehicles, and fancy clothes. The new group advocated change. So the difference continued.

That year on the farm at Spring Grove was short and full or bothersome incidents. Grandma grew worse. Pop did not seem at ease. Mom was busy with the family. One of my older brothers became ill with rheumatic fever and lay in a bed beside the largest and sunniest window in our living room, and my brothers who were well stirred up a lot of trouble with our friendly community tramp.

33

Irish Mik, as the tramp called himself, had been in our community long before I was born. He earned his meals and barn-lodging by splitting wood, mending fences, cleaning and greasing harnesses, and many other short-time jobs. A group of boys, including my brothers, angered him in his coffee den under the big trees along the creek west of the mill. His anger rose to murderous proportions. They teased him, called him names, pelted him with sticks and stones, and addressed him with threatening German expletives. In his rage he picked up a huge club.

"Get out," he called, "or I'll kill all of you."

"You couldn't do it."

"I'll show you," he responded as he started after them.

"You are too old and stiff. You can't run," challenged the boys.

"Look out," he shouted angrily.

"You old bum, you'll just fall over your own feet," they taunted.

Mik waved the club in the air high above his head and chased them all the way from the creek up through Bart Horst's wooded hillside, underneath the large horse chestnut trees in his yard. He was able to run much faster than they had expected. Gaining on them each step of the way, he followed them into our lane, wielding his big club and uttering threatening curses.

Pop was standing at the barn door. He saw the whole troop coming across Bart Horst's lawn. When the boys came into our barnyard, he stepped out to bring the chase to an end. Mik lowered his club and stopped his cursing, but he came all the way up to my father and made it very clear to him that if they ever tried anything like that again, they'd get hurt. Pop tried to allay his anger by offering him a warm supper, but Mik was too angry to accept the invitation.

During the winter Pop and Uncle Noah agreed to exchange places: Pop would take the Conestoga Mill and Uncle Noah the Spring Grove farm. When spring came, neighbors and friends joined us in the moving. It was a happy flitting. Both families moved in opposite directions. Uncle Noah's family was thrilled to be on the farm, and Pop was happy to be in the Conestoga Mill.

## CONESTOGA

It was mid-morning when our moving caravan arrived at Conestoga. Many of our relatives had already been at the house for some time, cleaning and planning for the placement of the furnishings.

When we disembarked from our carriage, Prince made an unexpected move and caused Mom to fall. She caught and broke her little finger in the carriage-seat hinges. Women in the house provided first aid. Pop rushed Mom to Doctor McConnell's office for proper treatment. When they came back everything was in place in our new home, and the women had a sumptuous meal ready.

Luke and I had spent the morning exploring in the new barn: hayloft, rafters, straw den, wagon sheds, and stables. In the hayloft I slipped and fell down on the hard floor in the horse stable. It knocked my breath away. By the time Luke came down the ladder to help me, I was up and breathing. We agreed to tell no one, but at the dinner table Luke went into great detail to tell every one.

The Conestoga Creek creeps along its beautiful banks through the most fertile fields of Lancaster County. The Conestoga Mill—a wooden structure, painted in soft light-blue—was situated in the center of that gorgeous Garden of Eden with Terre Hill and Bowmansville on the north and Blue Ball and Goodville on the south. A little, cabin-like structure with one small window on each side stood in the

36

center of the peak of the roof. It was the room for the head-shaft of the grain elevator. Its windows provided a far view of all the surrounding community.

A turbine provided power for all the machinery in the mill. An enormous gasoline engine stood ready to go into action in the event that water should run low or trouble develop with the turbine. Its flywheels stood higher than Pop's head. When it ran it created a thunderous noise. When it was shut down the silence was painful. It was an interesting, awesome thing. Though forbidden territory to me, I often pressed my face against the windows of the engine room and peered intently through the glass to watch the great engine run the big pulleys in the mill's powerhouse.

The house, covered with gray slate shingles, stood near the bank of the millrace about one hundred feet east of the mill. A porch spanned the west and south sides, the west side faced the mill. The south side stood parallel with the canal. The first floor provided a kitchen, dining room, living room, and two bedrooms. Grandma's room was the one facing the mill and the main road. Pop and Mom used the other. The rest of the family slept in large bedrooms upstairs. Added to the house on the east side was a structure that contained the family laundry, the creamery, a massive stone oven, and a tool shop.

Our house had two pieces of furniture that got special attention: one was the grandfather clock; the other an enormous, overstuffed, leather chair. The power for the clock was provided by two weights on chains and pulleys. Each night my father hoisted the weights from the bottom to the top to keep the clock going for another day. It struck the hour with a simple dong. Pop had purchased the chair from a famous mail-order store. It arrived in a large crate. When it was unpacked, we took turns sitting in it, but it was Pop's chair. He rested in it to heal his injured back.

The barn, standing at the end of the lane that ran between the house and the millrace, contained all the stables and sheds. From the barnyard a footbridge led across the race to a chicken house where thousands of white leghorn hens were kept.

A woodshed, painted red like all the other buildings except the house and the mill, stood directly across the lane from the laundry-house porch. It was built on posts and extended out over the race. Its windows provided an excellent place for fishing on rainy days. The wood and boards piled high against the walls provided fuel for the cook stove and the big, stone oven in the back wall of the laundry house. (Those boards also provided paddles for Pop in moments of special disciplinary care.)

Eli split wood for Mom in front of the shed. One cold, autumn morning he was chopping there before he went to school. A bad aim with the big ax split the end of his thumb wide open. It was a bloody cut, but Mom treated it and taped it so neatly and efficiently that he arrived at school before the last bell rang. The scar is still on his thumbnail.

Our flat-bottomed boat, painted blue to match the color of the mill, was moored beside, partly under, the woodshed. That boat carried us upstream and down, from one end of the millrace to the other. We stooped to pass under the high footbridge that joined the barnyard with the chicken house and rowed all the way up the channel to the main dam from which the canal drew its water. Halfway between the mill and the large dam, the race widened and formed a beautiful lake. Our farm lay on the north side of the lake. On the south bank, between the canal and the main stream of the Conestoga, stood our forest, splashing out its colorful leaves in all directions from early spring to late autumn. In the lake we learned to swim, dive, and hold our breath under water. Winter time brought skating and games of hockey to provide our recreation on the smooth, glistening ice that covered the lake. In the forest we gathered spring locust blossoms; in the fall, hickory nuts, walnuts, and chestnuts. There we watched the gray squirrels and red squirrels chase each other up and down the trees and from branch to branch, spied the rabbits scampering about in the thick undergrowth and the ground hogs caring for their young. Birds nesting in the trees were an added attraction.

At the heavy concrete breastworks beside the mill the water was deep. Beside the huge iron flood-control gates my older brothers had built a high diving-board. On summer evenings the place was crowded with swimmers and spectators.

Directly across the race from the woodshed there was an old water wheel. It was the source of continuous power for the laundry, the creamery, and the tool shop. A wire cable, running on pulleys, transmitted power to a shaft in the washhouse attic which in turn drove the machinery in the room below by means of belts and pulleys.

With its stacks of books and magazines that attic was the source of much entertainment, especially on rainy summer days. The gentle, monotonous sound of falling rain was many things to us, depending upon our mood. In contentment it was hypnotic and soothing. In frustration it was wearisome and even disgusting.

One day my mood was one of rebellion. I rolled on the attic floor in a wild delirium. Mom had warned me about the dangers of the revolving shaft and its belts and pulleys. But the temptation to roll back and forth under it overpowered me. Just to touch the revolving pulleys, the belts, couplings, and the cold, steel shaft seemed to take away the boredom. The set-screws in the coupling were especially fascinating. To feel their sharp edges as they turned round and round was great fun. But my boredom and my curiosity came to an end abruptly when one of the setscrews hooked onto the right leg of my overalls. A struggle with the ever-twisting, always-turning shaft and its coupling followed.

I could not escape from its clutches! In fear I screamed for help.

Susie and Mom rushed to the scene.

Isaac, working in the woodshed, heard me scream, and came running to the house.

"Bring me the butcherknife," Mom called to Susie.

"She's cutting his leg off," Katie cried when Mom took the knife from Susie's hand.

"No," Susie assured her.

Deftly Mom cut my pants free from the setscrews. Then all the machinery suddenly stopped. Isaac, with his new cap, had just whipped the cable of its pulley outside the attic window, tearing the cap to shreds.

\* \* \*

Paul, my youngest brother, was born on July 18, 1913, just about a month before I reached my fourth birthday. Harvey was then fifteen months old. Katie was in her seventh year, and Susie, Eli, and Edwin seemed very grown-up.

Susie and Katie had become intimate friends with many of the girls in our new neighborhood. One sunny, warm afternoon three girls came to our house to go boating. Susie's friends took the middle seat and did the rowing. Katie and her friend sat in the stern. Susie and I took the prow. The water was clear, and as the boat moved along we could see fish swimming about: sunnies, suckers, catfish, and carp. Bullfrogs, turtles, and water snakes crept among the leaves on the muddy bank. At the upper end of the race, the girls turned the boat around and started down stream. They drew the oars into the boat and floated with the lazy water.

From the boat we could see all the way up the gentle

slope to the fence and the trees marking our property line. The fields displayed yellow stubbles of a recently harvested wheat crop; a patch of dark-green potato stalks; clover in white, lavender, and blue; and corn, standing straight and tall, spreading wide its sea-green leaves. In the middle of the wide, shallow lake a large, long-legged crane was wading about feeding on small fish. We watched him in silence as the boat floated smoothly along in the warm sun.

Meanwhile, the crane moved about, slowly, intently, until our boat drifted into the range of his sight. Then his big wings raised his cumbersome body into the air, and he flew over the treetops and out of our sight.

Susie put her arms around me and drew me tightly to her side. A magic spell of happiness settled down upon us in the peace and beauty of our surroundings. As we drew closer to the big trees along the bank at the barnyard, Katie was unable to restrain her joy any longer. She stood up on her seat, clapped her hands, and jumped high to grasp a handful of leaves from the overhanging branches. She got the leaves, but the boat had drifted onward, and she fell splashing into the deep water. For a moment panic siezed us. Her friend could not reach her. Splashing and struggling, Katie whipped and beat the water with her arms and legs in a furious manner until she reached the shallow water near the bank. Dripping wet, she ran on ahead to the dock and helped us moor the boat under the woodshed.

*　*　*

Changes came quickly, affecting our surroundings and the way we lived. Strong men removed the heavy millstones, turned them upright, like gigantic wheels, and rolled them over the creaking floor to the main entrance. There they balanced them on heavy planks, then let them roll down to the ground. Cutting wide grooves into the mill

41

yard, they rolled across it to the hitching posts under the maple trees. There they toppled over and remained as relics of a bygone day.

Noah, a member of the New Weaverland Mennonite Church, had gotten a Studebaker truck. With it he did all of the hauling for the mill, and he established a daily run to Lancaster. On Sunday afternoons he took groups of young people on outings to Hershey Park, Willow Grove, and other places of interest.

The old covered bridge came under scrutiny. Highway engineers came upon the scene. They studied and measured the weather-beaten structure. Finally, as the engineers found shelter in the mill, a blast of dynamite brought the bridge down in a cloud of smoke, flying boards, and crackling timbers.

Then carpenters with heavy hammers and screaming saws moved in. They erected little shacks on the banks of the creek beside the mill. In those houses they stored their tools, ate their lunch, and one man, big Nick, slept there. Gasoline engines, concrete mixers, woodworking machines were running day after day. Big trucks brought heavy loads of lumber, sand, cement, stones and steel. After many months strong concrete walls stood in brilliant contrast with the blackish-gray boards and warped shingles of the covered bridge, which was now gone forever and lingered only in our memories.

The timbers and arches, the closely structured rafters, and the roof of that old bridge had formed a Sunday afternoon climbing cage for me and many other boys in the community. It was both thrilling and saddening to see the engineers destroy it in order to make room for one that would be safe for the increasingly heavy loads of automobile and truck traffic.

Much unrest and even division came into the Old Weaverland Mennonite Church because of the changes that were constantly taking place. Some people wanted to keep everything as it had always been. Others were eager to accept change. My father, as a businessman, had decided to make use of new machinery. This brought him into the center of the controversy. The bishops requested that he refrain from participating in the Holy Communion because of his involvement in worldly things. Some feared that sin from the big cities would be carried over the telephone and electric wires into our mill and home.

The New Weaverland Mennonite Church was different, and many in our family, as they grew up, joined that congregation. The new building stood diagonally across the road from the old one and at the bottom of the cemetery hill. The congregation sang hymns in the English language. Preachers used English in their preaching. They used telephones, automobiles, electricity, and new household and farm appliances. The Old Order Mennonites denounced all such innovations.

A strict Older Order deacon constantly afflicted the congregation with his harangue against the worldly practices of the new group, but in his own business affairs he dealt sharply. He required his farm hand to clean out all the barn stables on Sunday mornings. One Sunday morning the hired man decided to expose his boss. A group of prominent church people were going to have dinner with the boss and his family that day. When the carriages arrived there, the man was still deep in the manure. Surprise was expressed by the visitors that this good, strict leader in the church would have his employee working on Sunday.

The deacon was embarrassed!

"Quit this. Clean up and come in for dinner," he said.

"No, I don't feel well."

"Well, then quit. Put the wheelbarrow away and go to your room."

"No, I'll finish. I'll work slowly and get it done."

"This makes things look bad for me."

"I'm sorry about that."

"Let me take you to the doctor."

"No," the employee refused firmly.

"Well, you've got to stop this. You can't go on wheeling this manure out of the stables while all these church people are here for dinner." The deacon was angry. "Go up in the hayloft and sleep the rest of the afternoon," the deacon screamed.

"I'll finish the work. Just let me alone. I'll take my time to it. I'll be all right."

The deacon left the stable in utter exasperation. He joined his guests at the table and made no mention of the man with the wheelbarrow out on the manure pile.

The deacon was also a land shark. He used every trick in his clever brain to get more land, farm after farm. When the first World War came to an end, I was ten years old. Standing beside my Pop one day, I heard this prominent deacon say, "If this war would have lasted just a little longer, I could have bought my fourth farm."

*　*　*

My parents belonged to the Old Weaverland Mennonite Church and attended regularly. In sunshine, rain, heat, and cold, we attended services in that church on Sunday. The building was a quaint, massively stone-walled meeting house. After services we played with our cousins in that churchyard: It was hide-and-seek in the wagon sheds; skin-the-cat, chin-the-bar, and swing arms length at the hitching post railings; and sometimes a game of tag around the gravestones in the cemetery.

One cold, winter morning snowflakes were falling thick and fast. Our plain, black Mennonite carriage, with Prince patiently waiting, was at the yard gate. Susie placed the heated irons in heavy carpets and laid them in the carriage to keep our feet warm. Curtains were buckled down on all sides. Little glass windows provided visibility. We huddled close together, bundled in warm clothes and heavy blankets. Our Conestoga home was just a few miles away from the meeting house. At the church we settled down into our benches for the long singing and preaching session.

The interior of the sanctuary was divided into four main sections of wooden benches with scanty back supports. Two wide aisles intersected in the middle. I sat with Pop in the men's section. Susie, Katie, Harvey, and Paul sat with Mom in the mothers' part, facing the men's side. The singers, deacons, and preachers sat at the big table near the wall at the head of the aisle which separated the men and the women. The young people sat on the raised sections—boys and girls separated by the big aisle—facing the preachers.

The wind lashed and moaned at the corners of the building. Through the clear glass windows, we saw the dense snow swirling about. After dismissal a chill ran through the congregation as people wrapped themselves into their heavy coats and went outside. We stopped to face the blizzard and wade through the deep snow to the wagon shed where Prince, covered with his blankets, was waiting for us. At the church door we loaded the rest of our family into the carriage, buckled down the curtains, buried ourselves in the blankets, and shivered in our seats as Prince took us home through the deep and blinding snow.

\*　\*　\*

"Who wants to go for a ride in the bobsled?" Noah asked as we finished the noon meal.

"The girls must help with the dinner dishes first," Mom requested.

The snow was deep and still coming down.

Noah filled the bobsled with clean straw and hitched our

best horses to it. The girls did the dishes and called their friends to go along.

"Let's use the sleigh bells," Edwin suggested when the team was ready to go.

"No," Susie replied, "Mom wouldn't like that. The Old Orders think it's a sin to use sleigh bells. It's worldly!"

"It's not a sin," Edwin insisted. "The Old Orders are queer!"

"Well, Mom won't like it." Susie argued.

"Let's ask her," urged Katie.

Edwin ran in to the house while Noah got the bells ready.

"What did she say?"

"If there are to be harps in heaven, why not sleigh bells on the horses," he beamed.

"She did not say that," Susie declared.

"She did so." Edwin would not give up.

Eli helped Noah to buckle the bells on the horses.

Out from the shelter of the barn, the horses stepped high into the deep snow. They arched their necks and trotted vigorously in rhythm with the bells. The group sang and shouted as we passed the house and drove beyond the mill into the open road. Coming back home, the horses were tight on Noah's reins. Faster and faster they ran until we became frightened.

"We're going to have a wreck," Susie warned. "It's because we put the sleigh bells on!" She insisted. "It *is* a sin, and God is punishing us!"

"No," Edwin countered, "it's not a sin."

"Yes it is."

"No, the horses are feeling good and in a hurry to get home."

In silence Noah hung on to the reins as we went gliding through the blowing snow.

"The bells are sinful and worldly."

46

"No, they're not."
"Yes, they are."
"No."

## DEATH COMES TO OUR HOUSE

As spring of 1915 arrived, a solemn silence lay over our house. Grandma Gehman's waiting period was drawing to a close. Her body had suffered the ravages of cancer until it could endure no more.

"It's just a matter of time," Dr. McConnell said, "a few days or perhaps a week."

Every night someone ministered to her tired and restless body. We walked on tiptoe and whispered softly from morning until evening. On her last day the tension of expectancy ran high. My mind was filled with the question, "Is Grandma going to die today?" It was hard for me to imagine what it would be like to live without her. At the moment of her death I stood unnoticed in the ruffles of the drapery hanging in her bedroom doorway.

Doctor McConnell was standing beside Mom at Grandma's pillow. Henry had a long-handled fan in his hand and was moving it slowly back and forth above Grandma's face to relieve her feeling of suffocation. She stopped breathing. The doctor touched her eyes, her hands, and listened to her heart.

"She's gone," he said.

Tears filled Pop's eyes. He covered them with his handkerchief. Mom rose from her chair and kissed Grandma's forehead. At that moment Doctor McConnell saw me standing in the drapery of the doorway. He looked at Pop and pointed to me.

Pop looked at me and then at the doctor. "He's all right."

Mom laid a soft, white cloth on Grandma's face and drew the covers up to her chin. Then she drew all the window shades to darken the room.

The doctor put his things in his bag and snapped the buckles shut. When he had gone, our family gathered in the dining room. I sat at my place behind the table and leaned against the wall, feeling weak and lonely.

In a little while the mortician came. He worked in Grandma's room a long time. When he had finished and gone, we all went into the room to see Grandma's dead body resting motionlessly on a special couch which the undertaker had provided.

Our house was soon filled with people: neighbors, relatives, and friends who came to offer sympathy and assistance. On the day of the funeral all the folding chairs which the undertakers had stacked on our porch were in use by nine o'clock in the morning. All the rooms were filled with people and many stood outside on the porch and in the lawn. The bishop of the congregation took his place near Grandma's plain coffin and led the assembly in prayer and Bible reading. Other ministers offered comments of comfort. When the prayer service was ended, the funeral director placed the full-length lid upon the coffin and tightened it down with screws. Each screw screeched as it turned tightly on the coffin lid. I closed my eyes and wept.

Quietly the undertaker called the people to go to their carriages and line up for the procession to the cemetery. All moved in solemn dignity—fathers, mothers, and children, a grieving formation in black—from the house to the caravan of death. Then the morticians took their seat on the hearse. High and straight they sat on top of the gleaming, black death-wagon. We followed close behind them—all the way

49

out of the lane, over the bridge, and on to the cemetery. The sound of the slow, rhythmical hoof-beats of the horses, the crunching of the wagon wheels on the road, and the long procession of slowly moving carriages deepened the sadness of the occasion.

In the church yard the hitching posts and all the railings between them were already filled with teams. People were standing under the trees in large groups. Some had strolled into the cemetery. Others were standing beside Grandma's unadorned open grave.

Moving in measured steps, the funeral caravan went around the building to the main cemetery entrance. The carriages pulled into the reserved stalls. The hearse came to a halt in the great yard between the church and the cemetery. The coffin was placed on its stands in the shade of the large maple trees. The funeral director removed the screws from the lid. His helper laid it in the hearse. Then the multitude walked by to pay their last respects to the earthly remains of Grandma Susanna Sensenig Gehman, who died June 19, 1915 at the age of eighty-one years. The sunlight filtered down through the leaves of the trees. Shadows and light flickered on the dazzling white shroud, vivifying the undisguised pallor of death that rested unrelentingly on Grandma's quiet face. When our family walked by, Mom and Pop touched Grandma's hands and kissed her forehead. Tearfully Mom whispered, "The Lord Jesus is good to her. Now she is in peace."

Following my older brothers and sisters, I moved to the coffin and stretched to lay my hand on Grandma's. Her dead face mystified me. I thought of the morning when she said to me, "I'm just waiting for the Lord." I moved along with the family as I pondered that this day would bring to an end our earthly relationship with Grandma.

At the grave the coffin was placed on small planks until the preachers had said the final words of the ceremony.

Then the undertaker placed long, brown canvas straps under the coffin, one at each end, and gave them to the pall bearers. Quietly they lowered the coffin down into its rough box. When the rough box lid was in place, the grave diggers shoveled ground into the grave and filled it as the congregation sang. As the singing stopped, all followed the bishops into the church.

It was high noon when the preaching and the singing came to an end. In Christian sympathy and love many people joined us for the noon meal. At the table there was much conversation and laughter. I seemed to be the only one who couldn't eat. In quietness I left the table and sat in the woodshed by the window overlooking the millrace.

I went to bed that night with the odor of the morticians embalming fluid in my nostrils. The next day Mom and the girls scrubbed Grandma's room, changed the furniture, and aired the whole house, but the odor lingered, reminding me that Grandma was dead and that she was buried in the Weaverland Mennonite Cemetery.

## THE MAN WITH THE BROAD-BRIMMED HAT

I knew the man as one who practiced strict religious and economic austerity. I was afraid of him because of the strange stories my older brothers told about his ways and manners. He wore shabby, ragged clothes. His hat—a huge, dilapidated, broad-brimmed, dark-brown felt—fell down over his ears. His pants and jackets were homemade, loose fitting, and baggy. His Sunday clothes were made over the same pattern—flap pants and lapelless jackets. His Sunday hat was just like the one he wore during the week, though the brim was a little more firm. His hands were scabby, hard, knotted, and cracked from much hard work and exposure. His face was leathery and unshaven. He trimmed his whiskers with scissors because he regarded shaving as sinful. His eyes, brown and beady, were a little inflamed and watery most of the time. From both his nostrils there was a constant drainage. There was a big, red handkerchief in his hip pocket, hanging halfway out like a red flag.

This strange man never missed Sunday church services. He drove in an old carriage, and his horse wore the same harness on Sundays for going to church as he wore on week days for work in the fields. In church the man fell asleep and failed to use his red handkerchief. His jacket got soaked from the nasal drippings.

This man owned all the land around our place. He always wanted to buy one more farm, ours, and the mill. But

Pop would not sell them to him. His chickens, large Plymouth Rock hens and roosters, ran all over our place much of the time, feeding on grain that was spilled outside of the mill or on the floor inside.

One day Noah's little pigs broke out of their pen. He hunted for them everywhere on our farm and was not able to find them. Several days later our neighbor met him out under the big trees by the hitching posts near the old millstone.

"What happened to your little pigs, Noah?"

"I don't know. I can't find them."

"Well, I can keep them penned up, if you can't."

"You have my little pigs?"

"Yes, but I won't give them to you unless you promise to keep them in their pen."

"I promise."

Noah followed the broad, short-legged man behind his barn. A few minutes later they returned. Noah was carrying his little pigs under his arms.

"If it happens again, I'll keep them."

"It won't!"

Every Saturday evening after closing time this man would come into the mill by the lower side door and weigh for himself one hundred pounds of bran and one hundred pounds of chop, mark his purchase on a pad, tie his sacks, and load them on his wheelbarrow. The next week he would stop at Pop's office and pay for his Saturday evening self-service purchases.

"Does it bother you if I get my chop and bran this way?"

"Well," Pop said, "it would be better if you could come while we are still at the mill."

"Our work keeps us out in the fields so late," was his regular reply.

The next Saturday night Noah stayed in the mill, hiding in the engine room. At the regular time the lower door

53

opened and the man came in. When he was ready to leave, Noah appeared.

"I'll help you."

"Oh, no, that won't be necessary."

Noah weighed the sacks again and found that each weighed ten pounds more than the man had recorded.

"Look," Noah urged, pointing to the scales.

"I, I," the man stammered, "can't see too well. Isn't that one hundred pounds?"

"Look again."

"You read the scales. My eyes aren't very good."

"Each sack is ten pounds over the amount you marked on the pad."

"I must not do this any more. My eyes are just too poor."

Noah made the correction and helped the man to load the sacks on his wheelbarrow.

"I'll pay your Pop next week for all the mistakes I made." Then he pushed his wheelbarrow across the drive to his barn. He did offer to pay Pop for the numerous mistakes that he might have made because of his poor eyesight.

The next Saturday evening, however, he came fifteen minutes before quitting time with a bucket in his hand. He swept the scattered grain, bran, and chop from the floor and the corners of the bins and scooped it all up into his bucket.

"Why do you do that?" Noah asked.

"This will just be waste. My chickens will gladly eat these sweepings."

"So will my little pigs." Noah dumped the sweepings on the floor and gave the empty bucket back to the man. "If you wish to buy the feed, I'll gladly make out a bill for you."

The man took his empty bucket and went home.

About this time his wife looked everywhere for the big, brown eggs that her chickens laid: in our boxwood tree, behind the hydrangea shrubs, under our rose bushes, and all along the fence inside our yard. Several times each week she crept under our front porch. One evening as she was twisting and squirming out from under the porch, Noah met her at the porch steps. Her brown, leathery face blushed.

"My chickens hide their nests at the most difficult places."

"Indeed, they do."

"You charge so much for your feed that we can't afford to lose one egg."

"No, you must not lose one egg. Come in," he coaxed, "Mom and the girls will be glad to help you hunt in the cellar, in the coal bin, upstairs under the beds, in the closets, and even in our privy. Anywhere. We don't want you to lose one egg."

"I guess I made a pest out of myself." She moved toward our yard gate.

Noah stepped aside. "I'll promise to return any eggs that your big hens might lay on our property."

I loved to play in the sand under the big trees by the hitching post near the old millstone. I felt happy and free. One day without any warning a hand grabbed the seat of my pants and lifted me away from my toys.

"*Habst du nicht besser schaffen?*"

It was the neighbor's voice, and his big hand was pinching my bottom.

"*Ich spiele,*" I explained.

"*Schaffen ist besser!*" He swung me over his shoulder, carried me across the bridge to his big barn on the other side of the creek, and put me to work at the corn sheller.

I was afraid of the man.

The seat of my pants still seemed hot where his powerful fingers had pinched my skin. He turned the corn sheller crank. I stuffed the ears into it, and the shelled grains fell into a box on the floor. When the work was finished, he took me back to my toys.

Pop saw him. "What does all this mean"? he asked.

"A little work won't hurt the boy," the neighbor said.

"No, but you should not have taken him without telling me. How was I to know what happened to him?"

"I meant no harm. He ought to learn to work." Repeating his favorite, *"Schaffen ist besser, schaffen ist besser"* phrase, he insisted that he had done us a favor.

On another occasion the first floor of the mill was full of his chickens. Noah was chasing them out with a broom just as the man was coming in by the big double doors of the main entrance at the wide concrete steps.

"Do my chickens bother you?" he asked in utter innocence.

Noah looked at him soberly and said, "Yes, John, they're almost as bad as little pigs."

Chubby John lit up with a tricky, sheepish smile. *"Du bist en mann,* Noie. *Du bist en mann!"*

Chubby John had a very large family of fine children. They were farmers of the first degree. Their buildings, fences, fields, yard, and garden reflected great care in every detail. The same meticulosity characterized the beautiful, large, dark sandstone house in which they lived. They tolerated nothing inferior. They grew the most famous sweet-potato plants in the entire community.

Early one morning in planting season, a young man on horseback arrived for a basketful of those famous plants. His animal, a pretty, high-spirited sorrel, carried himself with magnificent conformation. Chubby John's sons watched as the rider put the horse through a variety of gaits in high style. After the performance the rider tied the horse to the family hitching post at the yard fence. Then he followed the neighbor's boys to the garden for the sweet-potato plants. To remount with the plants turned out to be

56

an impossibility. The horse would not stand still. Mike, one of the boys, tried to be helpful. He held the basket and reached out with it as the man rode by. But the horse wheeled, snorted, and kicked, striking Mike on the chest with such force that he and the plants flew back over the fence into the yard. Mike landed on the grass near the porch. He was unconscious. The doctor's examination revealed three broken ribs and cuts and bruises which were to confine Mike to his bed for a week or more.

The plants and the basket were gathered, and the young man came for them the next day in a buggy and with a different horse. He offered to pay the doctor bill, but Mike's father refused.

"It was an accident," he insisted, "an accident."

Many people came to see Mike, for he was everybody's friend. One evening I went with Eli to visit Mike. The boys often shared books and magazines. They even read novels, for neither Eli nor Mike agreed with the Old Orders which considered novels sinful. Novels were the work of the devil, the Old Orders believed, so Mike and Eli shared their books secretly. In a corner cupboard in Pop's office, on the highest shelf behind rarely used boxes, Eli hid his forbidden books. At Mike's bedside, Eli drew a book from the inside of his big shirt and gave it to him. Gratefully, Mike stuck it under his pillow.

Mike had another secret. He bought and sold Wrigley's Chewing Gum. He had received a new package that very day. His sister had sneaked it from the mailbox to his bedroom. It, too, was under his pillow, another forbidden thing. He gave me a piece of Black Jack.

"Do you like it?"

"Yeah, tastes like licorice candy."

"Look here," he said, opening his night shirt and pointing to the bruise marks on his chest. "You saw me going back over the fence, didn't you?"

"Yep."

"You were at the second floor door, weren't you?"

"Yep."

"Looked pretty bad, huh?"

"I thought it would kill you."

"So did I," he said as he covered the ugly marks.

Eli and Mike talked a while. I chewed my gum. Then we went downstairs. Mike's parents and his sister thanked us for coming. I held my chewing gum quietly in my mouth. Fortunately I had taken just a small part of the piece Mike gave me. The other part was in my pocket.

"Have some of my cookies and lemonade," Mike's sister said.

Chubby John invited us to sit down.

I looked at Eli and pushed my tongue against the side of my cheek.

He understood me, stretched his neck, and swallowed.

I got the message and swallowed the gum.

The cookies and lemonade were delicious.

When we left the house, it seemed like a different place to me. My boyish fear of Mike's parents was gone. I saw them as people who had love in their hearts the same as my parents had. I had felt friendliness coming from them.

## The Conestoga School House

The community school house stood along the East Earl road about a half mile from our house. My first teacher was a lovely, rosy-cheeked girl from the city of Lancaster. But she found it very difficult to communicate with the German-speaking beginners. She tried for a month or longer. Then one afternoon she began to scold. I cried. Others in the class cried. She cried. Her soft, lovely face became twisted and drawn as tears formed in her deep-blue eyes. Several weeks later she resigned. A German-speaking man came to take her place. That made a great difference for me and others like me. He explained things to us in our language. In a short time a new world began to open in my mind—the world of letters, reading, and books.

One evening Susie's closest friend held my hand as we walked home from school with the ten or twelve pupils going our way. At the place where she had to leave our group, she stooped and put her arm around me.

"I love you," she said, "and I want to take you home with me tonight."

The girl was extremely beautiful. Completely swept away with feelings of love for her, I looked at Susie.

She shook her head firmly.

The girl kissed me on the cheek. I was transfixed in her arms and pleaded with Susie.

"No."

59

"Well, we can walk together tomorrow evening," the girl said.

That night sleep overtook me as my thoughts were filled with reveries of love: the lovely face, warm arms, and the kiss on my cheek. On several Saturday afternoons Susie took me to her friend's home. Susie never told Mom about my passionate love affair with her closest girl friend.

Roy Burkhart, a neighbor of ours, was in my class. His family lived in Chubby John's house across the creek from our place. Roy's parents spoke both English and German. He learned fast. I was far behind him, but when I learned to read and understand English, I soon caught up with him. All through the years of our Conestoga School life, Roy and I were rivals for the head place in class.

* * *

Still, I loved the mill!

The restful, humming, tranquilizing sound of smoothly running machinery; the sight and scent of pure white flour; the sweet odor of fresh corn meal; the taste of new bran, and the coming and going of customers made life at the mill very fascinating.

One night danger seemed to arise.

At two o'clock in the morning the house telephone began to ring. Pop was awakened and answered. Soon my brothers and sisters were awake and downstairs.

"What's wrong?"

"What happened?"

"Did somebody die?"

Questions came from all sides.

"The telephone operator says somebody is using our phones at the mill," Pop explained.

When they left the house with their guns in their hands, it seemed as though a very fearful thing might happen.

"Don't shoot," Mom called after them as they went out

into the dark. "It's a sin to kill. We must help him, not hurt him."

"We'll just scare him," Pop assured her. "We'll walk around the mill a couple of times. If we hear and see nothing, we'll go inside and take a good look."

Mom and the girls and I sat on the couch in the living room. Mom talked about praying, loving enemies, feeding the hungry, doing good to those who hate you, and turning no one away who asks for help. Then she told us to go back to bed, get our sleep and rest, and be ready for school in the morning. On our way upstairs Susie whispered into Katie's ear.

"What did you say?" I asked.

"Nothing."

"Yes, you did. Tell me too."

"Oh, I just said that we should make him a good, warm breakfast, if they catch him."

"I think so too," Katie said. "Mom said we must do good to those who cause trouble for us."

"No, he must go to jail," I insisted. "He's doing wrong."

"We must return good for evil. We must provide for the strangers and for those who have no friends. The Bible says that's what we must do." Susie spoke with authority.

"Well, I hope they put him in jail too."

The next morning at the breakfast table all the details were explained. Nothing was molested inside or outside of the mill. There were some strange tracks on the fifth floor. They led up to the little cabin on top of the roof. The window on the south side of the cabin was open, a piece of a man's coatsleeve was caught on a nail at the side of the window frame. The intruder might have escaped that way and made his way down to the ground by climbing into the branches of the big tree at the south gable-end of the mill.

The community constable watched the mill for several days and nights. No disturbance of any kind was repeated.

However, a few days later we got word that a demented neighbor, who had been hospitalized in the Lancaster Hospital for the Mentally Disturbed, had escaped. He had made several appearance in the homes of his closest friends. He always appeared quietly and left suddenly, leaving people surprised and bewildered. He was at his own home for a few days. Then the authorities returned him to the hospital. Perhaps he had caused the disturbance in our mill.

For several days the story of the demented man was told and retold on the playground of the Conestoga School.

"He just walked into Graybill's kitchen without knocking. He sat on a chair for a few minutes. Then he got up and left without saying a word."

"Yes, at Horning's he hid in the barn one night."

"At our place he sat on a stool in the milk house."

"He came into our kitchen, sat on the woodbin beside the stove, and watched Molly prepare supper. Mom invited him to eat with us. He shook his head but never said a word. In a little while he got up and walked out. Mom called his wife and told her. She told Mom that they were looking for him."

"Will they send him back to the hospital?"

"I guess so."

"I'd be afraid to live with a man like that."

"He wouldn't hurt anybody."

"He just sits around quietly."

"Not always."

"I'll say not. They took him to the hospital in the first place because he had gotten so angry and violent that he broke up a lot of furniture and threatened to kill his wife."

"He seems very quiet and harmless now."

"But no one can tell how soon he might get another one of those spells."

"I think they should take him back to the hospital as soon as they can catch him."

62

"I bet he was the fellow who got into the mill."

"My Pop thinks so."

Until he was returned to the hospital, the man was the object of our fears and conversations on the playground. Even the teacher seemed relieved when word came to us that our demented neighbor was safely returned to his room in the asylum.

\* \* \*

The Conestoga School was a simple one-room, wooden structure, painted blue like the mill, and it had white shutters on the windows. A big, pot-bellied stove stood in the middle of the room. Older pupils carried water from a neighboring farm and buckets of coal from the school basement. At recess and lunch the playground rang with happy voices as the see-saws went up and down, baseballs or snowballs flew over the fences, and tag-rings flashed with long skirts and high-laced shoes.

"Would you like to make a lot of money by catching *elbedrichlin*?" an older boy, who always stood at the foot of his reading class because he couldn't read a word without help from the teacher, asked a group of younger ones.

"How do we catch them?" they all asked.

"You stand at the corner of a building on a day when a very cold wind is blowing. You take a burlap bag and hold it open in the wind. The wind will blow the *elbedrichlin* in."

"Do we get a lot of money?"

"More than you would for muskrats, skunks, or even more than you would get for possom or raccoon hides."

"Do they bite?"

"No, they can't bite you."

"What do they look like?"

"You can't see them, not outside, just indoors."

"Will you show us how to catch them?"

"Yes, I'll bring the right kind of bag along tomorrow and

then when a cold wind blows, I'll show you how to hold the bag."

The cold, windy day came and the boy was successful in freezing several of us in the icy blast behind the school before the teacher became aware of his trick. One of the boys, the third in the group that volunteered, was crying and shivering beside the pot-bellied stove inside the building.

"What's wrong?" The teacher looked at the three boys huddled close to the stove.

"We're freezing."

"Why did you stay out so long?"

The boys looked at one another and remained silent.

"Tell me."

"Catching *elbedrichlin*."

"What?"

"*Elbedrichlin*."

"*Elbedrichlin*?"

"Yes, *elbedrichlin*."

"Why were you trying to catch *elbedrichlin*?"

"To sell the hides and make a lot of money."

The fourth boy came in shivering.

"Where is Johnny Schnupps?" The teacher's voice was stern.

"He's in the privy behind the wind, showing us how to catch *elbedrichlin*."

"Bring him in."

The biggest boy in school went out to get him.

Johnny Schnupps came in.

"Johnny, why did you do that?"

Johnny's face produced a diabolical smile. His shoulders screwed around his neck, and his lips twisted into a scowl.

"Johnny, you're cruel, making these boys believe that they can catch *elbedrichlin* in the cold wind. What if they catch colds instead? What if they get sick?"

Johnny's scowl faded from his face. "They didn't have to do it," he said.

"No, but it was still a very mean trick."

Johnny hung his head.

"For the next week you will spend every recess and every noon writing the word '*elbedrichlin*' on the blackboard."

\* \* \*

Isaac made an evening trip on horseback for Pop. On his way home in the dark, a darting wild animal frightened the horse, causing him to rear to the side of the road. Unprepared for the sudden careening, Isaac fell and struck his head on a stone.

"Something must have happened to Isaac," Mom said. "He should be home by now."

"He'll be all right," Pop said, and continued reading his newspaper.

"I'm worried. It's taking him much too long." Mom went to one window after another and looked out into the dark.

"Maybe he met a friend," Susie consoled.

Mom sighed. "I'm still worried," she said. "I have a feeling that something went wrong."

We all knew that Mom's feelings were not to be taken lightly.

Mom thought she heard a shuffle in the lane and opened the big door to the porch.

"Is this Sammy Gehman's house?"

"It's Isaac," Mom said and went out on the porch.

Pop laid his newspaper down and followed.

We all crowded to the open door.

The horse stood motionless at the yard gate.

"Easy, Ben," Pop said as he took the bridle reins.

Eli held the bridle as Pop lifted Isaac from the horse and kept on assuring him that he was now at home.

"Is this Sammy Gehman's house?" Isaac mumbled constantly.

Eli took Ben to the barn.

Pop carried Isaac into the living room and laid him on the couch. Mom went to get towels and a basin of warm water. Together they washed the thick, sticky blood from Isaac's hair, neck, and shirt. When Pop saw the deep cut, he gave the wet towel to Mom, went to the telephone, and called Doctor McConnell.

The doctor came late. Isaac was still delirious.

The doctor treated the ugly gash, stitched it, and gave Isaac medicine to relieve his pain.

A logging camp near our mill was the scene of a tragic accident one wintry day. Eli and Edwin were close friends of the neighbor's sons who worked at the camp. They often visited and sometimes helped with the work there. They fastened the cable to the logs at the bottom of the hollow near the creek bank, and the owner's boys operated the powerful, steam-driven winch at the top of the hill where the sawmill stood. One morning the cable broke and its backlash hit the young winch operator on the head and tore his brains out. He died instantly with his hands on the winch controls.

Another neighbor was found dead in his bedroom. He had hanged himself with a rope. He had come to our mill every week. We bought his wheat, oats, and corn. Pop did all his grinding for his large herd of animals. His family carriage often followed ours as we drove to and from the Weaverland Mennonite Church. I played with his boys in the churchyard after services.

Troubles seemed numerous. The greatest had come when the United States declared war on Germany in 1917. The daily question clouding our house was "will our boys have to take military training and go to war?" Discussions about it at the table made me too sick to eat. I always sought solace and peace in the woodshed by the open window overlooking the millrace.

My deepest anguish grew out of our Mennonite commitment to the ways and teachings of Jesus. The war was a challenge to those teachings. "All war is sin," the preachers proclaimed. To take part in it was disobeying Jesus. To disobey Jesus was incomprehensible. How could anyone, any nation or nations, be so callous?

Funerals, funerals, funerals, an uncounted number of them occurred during our last winter at Conestoga. The war and the flu made death a daily topic. Its miserable complications—fever, sweating, chilling, bodily aches and pains that reached unbearable proportions—struck us down one by one. But as funerals went by our house, we watched from the windows, and slowly made our own recovery. Neither the war nor the flu took any from our family. The war did not reach us because all my older brothers were conscientious objectors to it and any phase of participation in it. The flu made us all very sick but none died.

The war, though, brought to an abrupt end our lovely, exciting, and beautiful life on the banks of the Conestoga. When the government agents appeared and told Pop that he had to manufacture flour and other feeds in keeping with their directives, he obeyed, but he got out of the milling and feed business as soon as possible.

Our property, mill, farm, and all, was up for sale!

Our world was falling to pieces!

The machinery of the mill would be silenced. The freedom of the meadow and the millrace would be gone. Its variety of summer life and color—snakes, fish, birds, turtles, and wild animals would disappear. Its winter death-like silence under the deep, glistening whiteness of ice and snow would no longer stimulate my sense of sound and sight. The community of customers would come no more.

* * *

We were truly children of the Conestoga, growing to a good start in life in the picturesque, natural simplicity of the land along its banks. Most of the family stayed within easy reach of those alluring childhood surroundings. Henry found employment in New Holland. Jacob turned to farming, Samuel to the automobile business, Noah to trucking, and Isaac to farming. They established their own homes only minutes away from Mom and Pop.

Similar in height, weight, and appearance, our fair complexion, light-brown hair, blue eyes, and German accent betrayed our heritage. Some difference appeared as time went on. Eli and Susie were mild mannered with good health and kind, affectionate attitudes. They could never work away from home even for one summer because homesickness overpowered them. Noah and Katie were the more peaked among us, but they were tough in mind and spirit and battled to keep their place in life. Samuel was the quiet one. His silent way of going about his work was baffling to many. Edwin was the most aggressive and outgoing. His exuberant readiness to defend his rights sometimes led him to the brink of conflict. Jacob was the great toiler; and Henry, the intellectual.

In a field one day with a team of three horses, things went wrong for Noah. The horses were sluggish and Noah's mood vile. He yelled, jerked, and beat the animals until they became demoralized as a team, and, tangled up in each others traces, they went totally out of control. Pop came upon the disarray just as Noah was at the height of a cursing rage. The two men faced each other in silence: Pop with calm eyes looked into Noah's angry face. Several suspense laden moments passed by. Then Pop turned back toward the mill and walked from the field. At the fence he turned and said, "Noah, the horses might understand you better if you were to talk to them in German." Noah was dumbfounded! He sat down in the middle of the chaos that he had created and cried.

Henry and Jacob, in addition to their regular employment, were part-time tobacco growers on Uncle Noah's Spring Grove farm. It was a tedious, year-round toil, requiring maximum care in seeding, transplanting, cultivating, fighting pests, harvesting, curing, and stripping. But many tobacco growers became wealthy.

The stripping room in the winter time was often a place of long hours of work and hilarity. Uncle Noah was gifted with a very subtle sense of humor. His tricky games stimulated a fascinating give-and-take and filled the days with fun. He rigged doors with buckets that dumped water, straw-chaff, or ashes on the next person going through. Henry was determined to out-do his clever uncle. He removed the pellets from a shotgun shell, shortened and reloaded it with gunpowder only, and rigged it in the tobacco cellar in a way that would discharge the gun when Uncle Noah got his next batch of tobacco for processing in the stripping room.

The scheme worked!

Noah drew his tobacco from the tier. The gun went off, creating a deafening sound under the low ceiling spanning the heavy stone walls of the cellar. Uncle Noah dropped to the floor with his armful of tobacco and began to moan as though seriously wounded. Henry and Jacob listened. Was Uncle really hurt? He was moaning and squirming on the floor. What did it mean? The moaning continued. They walked into the cellar with puzzled, sober faces. But when they came to Uncle Noah, he jumped up with his tobacco, laughing heartily. A few minutes later, at work in the stripping room, they all agreed to quit the stunt stuff.

* * *

"Where's my kitten?" Katie cried at cat feeding time.

"Oh, maybe she went for a long walk," Mom said. "She'll be back tomorrow."

Katie called and called her cat the next day at feeding time, but the cat did not appear.

"She'll come back," Mom reassured her again.

"My kitten is not here," Katie complained.

"She'll come back."

"I'm afraid she won't."

Each day we went through the same crying routine, but Katie's kitten did not come back home. I knew where her cat was, that she had not gone on a long walk, and that she would never come back. Each day the horrible feeling of being the cat killer went deeper and deeper into my conscience. As the calling and crying routine intensified, my guilt feelings grew more powerful. I could retain them no longer.

"Mom, I must talk to you," I said as Katie was calling and crying.

"What?"

"I killed Katie's kitten."

"You killed her kitten?"

"The cat scratched me, and I hit her with a stick. It killed her. Then I tied a big stone to her body and threw her in the race. She's dead. She'll never come back."

"Why didn't you tell Katie?"

"I was afraid. I knew she'd get cross and fight."

"Shall we tell her now?"

"Yes."

Then the delicate skill so common to Mom's way guided us through a long session of hysterical crying, accusations, and apologies.

\* \* \*

Sometimes Mom was very severe!

During his first year in school Eli was very quiet and bashful. He did not like going to school and got out of it whenever possible.

"What was that crashing noise in the washhouse?" Mom asked her kitchen maid.

"I don't know. May's doing the laundry."

"The children all went to school, except these little girls." Susie and Katie were playing on the kitchen floor at Mom's feet. "I'd better take a look. That Eli might just be trying to sneak out of school again."

Eli had hidden in the laundry room instead of following the older boys to school. He waited until the wash maid was out hanging up the clothes. Believing himself to be unnoticed, he made his way to the corner shelf and began to play with the old clock that stood on top of it. It did not run, but when it was wound properly, it struck the hour. Eli was going to make it strike as he had seen Isaac and Edwin do. He opened the clock door, wound it, and was in the process of moving the big hand around to the striking point, when the clock slipped from the shelf and crashed to the floor.

"Eli!"

He looked up from his work of hiding the pieces.

"Now, you get a spanking; then off to school with you."

Mom held Eli's arm and whipped him soundly as she pushed him across the porch and off to school.

Eli tried to explain.

Mom would not listen. "Off to school with you, and don't you ever try a trick like that again."

Eli went, but he held his face shut all day and never said a loud word in class all year.

* * *

"What's in that bucket?"

"This bucket?" Isaac held the bucket out, urging Mom to take a look.

"What's in it?" Mom wouldn't look. She knew.

"Fish," Isaac explained.

Mom's blue eyes widened. "Fish?" she inquired and studied Isaac's face earnestly.

He blushed and became hot all over. "The bucket is nearly full. Big fish. They'll make several meals for our whole family."

"Those fish? Meals for our family? By no means! At this house we don't eat fish caught on Sunday!" She calmly looked at her boy who had gone fishing instead of to church. Then she said, "You take those fish right back and dump them into the creek.

* * *

"Take your pants off. Get behind the stove and stay there until they are dry."

Eli's face was blue cold. Against Mom's better judgment, he had gone skating on ice that was not strong enough to hold him.

"You'll break through," she had warned.

"I'll test it and be careful."

The kitchen was full of visiting women and children. The men were in the living room, discussing the morning sermon. It was a custom among the Old Order Mennonites to gather in homes after Sunday preaching, enjoy a lavish dinner, and then spend the afternoon talking. The women talked family matters. The men discussed the morning sermons to the best of their ability. Sometimes the discussions ran into heated arguments. Eli cared very little about listening to either group, and he was old enough to enjoy the winter out-of-doors. But now he stood in front of the stove

72

in the presence of all those women and children, and his pants were frozen stiff up to his waist.

"Behind the stove with you and stay there until they're dry." Mom didn't say another word. She pointed her finger at the space behind the stove.

*   *   *

"Katie is taking my wagon."

"No, I'm not."

"Yes, Mom, she is. Make her stop it."

"Children, children, behave."

Mom was in the kitchen. She didn't leave the stove. Katie kept on pulling my wagon away from me while I was loading it with blocks.

"Stop it," I screamed and began to kick her. I grabbed her hair and pulled. Then she screamed.

Mom came into the living room and reached to give me a paddling. I struck her hand and ran for the door. She came after me. I slammed the door in her face, and the window glass crashed to the floor under Mom's feet.

"You ugly boy," she said and came over the glass after me.

But I was already out in the lane and on my way to hide in the barn.

"Pop will see you about this," she called after me. "You are an ugly boy."

In the barn I crept far under the wagons and grumbled as I crept, "It was Katie's fault. She started it." However, having Mom think of me as an ugly boy bothered me, and I began to feel miserable about the incident. It was very dark under the wagons. Rats crawled and squealed in the corners. I saw them in the light that filtered through cracks in the boards. In a few minutes I decided to return to the house and ask Mom to give me a spanking.

"Mom, give me a spanking. I didn't want to be an ugly boy."

She was busy at the kitchen sink and didn't turn to look at me. "You go out to the mill and tell Pop what happened."

Her statement was shocking and final.

I stood alone!

"Tell Pop." The words rang in my ears.

The fatal moment would arrive no later than dinner time. Hesitating at different places, I made my way slowly toward the mill, asking myself, "Which shall it be? Now or later?" I sat on top of the concrete stairs at the main entrance and looked back at the big millstones under the trees. The grooves they had made were still noticeable. I imagined what a whipping from Pop's hand feels like. I remembered the sting, the fire, and the lingering, burning sensation. In a kind of dazed condition, I entered the mill and walked slowly to Pop's side at the flour packer. His clothing, hands, and face were white with flour.

"What's wrong?" he asked moments later.

"Nothing," I replied and remained standing at his side.

He resumed his work. After a long while he stopped the machine, stooped, put his arm around me, and drew me close to his side. "Tell me, what's wrong?"

"You must give me a whipping."

"Why, what did you do?"

"Mom said I was an ugly boy."

"She did?"

"Yes."

"Were you?"

I told Pop the whole story.

He looked at me soberly.

"You must give me a whipping." The suspense was oppressive. He seemed baffled. I had expected a vigorous spanking, but now he was hesitating and looked puzzled.

"Can you tell Mom and Katie that you're sorry?"

"I did."

"Can you tell me?"

"Yes, I don't want to be an ugly boy. I'll never do it again."

He gave me a quick hug. "This afternoon we'll get a new piece of glass and fix that door so that no one will ever know that the glass was broken. You and I will fix it together."

Not a word was said about the broken glass at the dinner table.

"There, now," Pop said, "the door is as good as new." He opened and closed it and examined it very carefully on both sides. "No one can see that the glass was broken, and we'll tell no one what happened here this morning."

*  *  *

"Mom, Mom, a snapper is biting my leg."

Mother laughed and tried to assure Susie that she was not being attacked by a big snapper.

"You just laugh," Susie scolded. "It is a snapper, and he will bite my leg off."

"Well, hurry. Swim faster." Mom had encouraged both Susie and Katie to swim farther out into the deeper water. They had expressed fear.

"I'll sink," Katie said.

"No, you won't sink. Just keep your arms over the piece of wood. It will keep you floating. Then kick and paddle. That way you will be able to swim far without even getting tired."

The girls had made their way far upstream, when Susie's sudden fear gripped her.

"A snapper, a snapper. He's biting my leg."

Mom could not believe that a snapper was threatening Susie's safety.

"Hurry, hurry, paddle and kick faster. Get away from him."

Susie engaged in vigorous splashing that sent a misty spray up around her. When she came to shore, there were no marks on her legs.

"See," Mom said, "it was not a snapper; just little fishes nibbling at your legs. Go back into the water and swim."

\* \* \*

Jonas Schnitzle had turned into a very wicked young man, defying his parents, the church, and God. He drank heavily, spent many nights at sinful places, and caused his family much grief.

"He is demon-possessed," someone said."

"I'm worried," his mother cried. "He's sick, not demon-possessed."

"It's the devil who's causing him to behave so."

"No," his father replied.

"He's sick," his mother said. "We must put him in the hospital. He's out of his mind. He doesn't know what he's doing."

"The devil can take possession of a fellow."

Jonas had been brought home from town and was upstairs in his room. He was screaming, bellowing like a bull, grunting like an angry boar, braying like a mule, and crowing like a rooster. Then he pounded the walls and kicked the furniture.

"It is the devil!"

"No."

"Poor boy, he wouldn't do that, if he were himself."

"It's the devil. That's how people act when they are demon-possessed."

"Ask Sammy Gehman to phone for the doctor. He has telephones. He'll do that for us." Jonas' mother was in

76

tears. She walked around in the kitchen, wringing her hands. "Poor boy; the poor boy must be so sick."

The doctor came late at night.

Jonas cursed and threatened to kill any one who dared to enter his room.

"Tomorrow you must take him to the insane asylum," the doctor said. "He is very dangerous."

The doctor and Jonas' parents stood at the bedroom door and listened as Jonas cursed, threatened, brayed, crowed, bellowed, and pounded.

"This medicine would quiet him down a little, I think, if we could get him to take it."

"He won't let us in," his father said.

"He'd kill us, if we went in," his mother said.

"Even if we could hold him, he wouldn't take the medicine. He's a hospital case," the doctor concluded.

The troubled parents were spared the pain of taking their son by force to the Lancaster Insane Asylum. In a cursing, storming rage, he died before morning.

On the day of the funeral, the churchyard was filled with people at the Old Weaverland Mennonite Church. A solemn mood lay over the cemetery hill and all the churchyard.

"He was possessed by the devil," people whispered.

"Isn't it terrible. His poor parents."

"If it happened to him, it could happen to anybody."

"Yes, I guess it could."

"Do you really believe the devil caused him to be that way?"

"I think his Mom is right. He was not at himself. He was out of his mind."

"He was crazy."

"Isn't that the same as being possessed by the devil."

"I don't think so. Being crazy is a sickness of the mind."

77

"The devil can cause people to be sick."

"Does he cause rheumatism?"

"Did he cause the flu?"

"What about your cold?"

"Or your stomach trouble?"

After the preaching, the people left the churchyard in solemn, fearful moods. In our carriage the discussion continued. Mom allayed the fears that had been aroused in us by the informal talk around the gravestones. Her simple statement of faith was "If we love and obey Jesus, the devil cannot harm us," she said. *Der schlecht mann* has no power in the presence of *Der Gut Mann*."

## East Earl

During the winter Chubby John bought the Conestoga Mill and the farm from Pop. In the spring of 1919 we moved to our new home on a farm near East Earl. The community was still in the grip of the flu epidemic. Funerals went by our place several times a week. At one place two men died on the same day. It seemed as though the great nightmare of sickness and death was starting all over again. The terrible disease struck me a second time, and before it cleared away the infection affected my eyes.

"Keep him in a dark room," the doctor said, or he may go blind."

I had overheard the doctor's conversation with my parents in the hall outside of my bedroom door. My thoughts swam in a great ocean of fear. For weeks Mom had helped me to eat, drink, and perform my elemental needs in total darkness with thick bandages over my eyes. Emptiness, blindness, nothing! I was afraid of the day when the doctor would remove the bandages. Almost I hoped it would never come!

On the scheduled day the doctor's car came into our lane. My heart raced. My lungs seemed tight with excitement. The fear that I would never be able to see again was oppressive.

The light! How wonderful it would be to see the light without pain!

The doctor removed the bandages.

"Open the window shades just a little," he said to Mom. "Now open your eyes. Just a little blink."

I did.

"Could you see the light?"

"Yes."

"Did you have any pain?"

"No."

"Blink again, several times, slowly. Keep your eyes open just a little longer."

I followed the doctor's instructions.

"Any pain?"

"No."

"Good! Now I want you to look at me."

Mom and Pop were standing close by the doctor's side.

"Can you see me?"

"Yes," I cried.

"Can you see Mom and Pop?"

"Yes, I can see them too." I cried. An inner happiness seemed to swell.

"Now close your eyes and let them rest a little."

"I'm not blind." I closed my eyes.

"No," the doctor said, "your eyes seem to be all right."

We rested in silence a few minutes.

"Open the shades a little more."

Mom followed the doctor's directions and adjusted the shades as he requested.

"Open your eyes again."

I did. I could see the furniture in the room, the pictures on the wall, and even the designs on the wallpaper.

"Very good," the doctor said, "but now we'll put the bandages on again and darken the room. Tomorrow we'll try again. So far things look good."

Within a month the doctor declared my recovery complete.

When school opened, I was ready to attend with Harvey and Paul. Susie and Katie stayed at home to help with work on the farm. School at Cedar Grove was quite different from Conestoga. The building was new and modern. The heater in the corner of the room, almost out of sight, was covered with ornamental sheet metal. At lunch time, in cold weather, we gathered around it to toast our sandwiches over the hot coals with long-handled toasters.

We were the only German-speaking boys in school. The other pupils called us "The Dutch Boys." Together we faced a trying situation. We had no close playmates and were the objects of ridicule on many occasions. On the playground our new schoolmates often cornered us with cruel invectives, making fun of our Dutch speech, Dutch clothing, Dutch glasses, and Dutch religion.

Our East Earl farm lay in the valley at the foot of Sheep Hill, a portion of the Welsh Mountains that stretch from New Holland to Downingtown. The Downingtown-Lancaster branch of the Pennsylvania Railroad ran along the northwest side of our land. New Holland was four miles to the west, Cedar Lane one half mile east, Blue Ball and Terre Hill to the north, and the hills and valleys of the Welsh Mountains to the south.

This farm provided the ground upon which we, as children of the Conestoga, grew to our years of youthful maturity. Here we struggled with every problem known to growing youngsters. On this farm we made the transition from the freedom of early childhood to hour after hour of purposeful toil in sun and storm, in heat and cold, and in loss and gain. Still, there were times, when the work was done, for play and creative fun and pleasure.

* * *

"Stop that, stop it!" Harvey yelled at the top of his voice. But I couldn't stop. It was too much fun.

81

"Will you stop that?" The voice came from the house.
Pop came out of the kitchen door and bore down upon
me with great strides.

I had been the toymaker for the three of us—Harvey,
Paul, and myself. I made wagons, trucks, locomotives,
barns, houses, mills, and the like. In the orchard behind the
huge tobacco shed, we built our little village. When any
new toys were needed or repairs had to be made, we returned to the carpenter shop in the tobacco shed. Saws,
planes, hammers, hatchets, drawknives, levels, awls, pliers,
wrenches, sanders, vises, and grinders were within easy
reach.

I made three wooden guns—lock, stock, and barrel—and
equipped each one with a spring taken from old window
shades. A nail in front of the broomstick—the barrel—provided a hook for the spring. Properly hooked and stretched,
it would fly fifty or sixty feet.

Harvey's spring lodged behind the shutter of one of the
tobacco cellar windows. When he went behind the shutter
to get it, I shot my spring against the shutter. To my surprise, it bounced back to me. I shot it against the shutter
repeatedly.

"Stop it," he screamed at the top of his voice.

My spring flew back and forth as fast as I could manage
to make it go.

"Pop, Pop, make him stop it."

In seconds Pop grabbed the gun from my hands and
whipped me with the stock end of it until it broke into
splinters and nothing remained but the broomstick.

Pop let go of my arm without a word and returned to the
house to finish his breakfast. I crept deep into the narrow
crevice between the chicken house and the tobacco shed
and remained there until Eli called and persuaded me to
come in for the noon meal.

"Harvey, did you make that truck?"

Harvey smiled with swelling pride.

"It's beautiful."

"And look how neatly he has painted the lines on it."

"I can't believe it."

"You're going to be a good mechanic someday, Harvey. That is very fine craftsmanship." Henry, my oldest brother who was the chief pattern-maker for the New Holland Machine Company, had just joined the circle of admirers of Harvey's work. "I'll have to keep my eye on you. Keep that up and you'll get a job in my department at the machine company."

In our own carpenter shop, Harvey had followed my patterns. He used my ideas. But he did more precise work. He painted his toys in beautiful color, making clean, straight lines. My woodwork was rough. My paint jobs smeared.

As the whole family smothered him with admiration, I began to feel a dark, torturesome jealousy awaken within me. I wanted to beat him with my fists and smash his truck into sawdust. The feeling of jealousy was most oppressive. I brooded in envious darkness until misery totally overpowered me. But light broke through my darkness again. Harvey's work was better than mine! Any person could see that at a glance. A question exploded in my mind: "Do *I* have the honesty and courage to appreciate his skill and praise him for it?"

\* \* \*

Jacob had moved on a farm at Pool Forge near Churchtown. In the summer of my eleventh birthday, I worked for him on that farm. My pay was ten dollars a month. I helped with the feeding, milking, stable work, and regular work in the fields. The work days were long—from sunup to sundown, and weariness grew so acute that my dreams seemed to be a continuation of the day's toil.

Three other men worked on that farm. Clayton Leed was

Jacob's main employee. He was a good worker, a well-built, stocky person, and good natured for the most part. But he suffered mild epileptic convulsions. When the attacks came upon him, he stood still for a few seconds and moaned and shuddered. The ailment, though, was sufficient to ruin his marriage. His wife divorced him and married another man. He talked to me, almost daily, about his unhappiness. He described vividly the troubles and dissatisfactions that broke up their marriage.

His unhappiness was oppressive to me. I often wished that he had not told me. Still, in the light of what I saw going on between male and female animals on the farm, I was able to understand, at least in a small way, the disappointment that he felt.

Rebecca, Jacob's wife, provided room and board for her brother Jonathan. He was mature, single, very handsome, and had traveled extensively in the United States in his automobile. With his car, his stories of travel, and the smoke of his cigarette curling out of his mouth or blowing from his nose, he seemed like an idol. His younger brother Abram and I worshipped him. But one Sunday afternoon Jonathan tossed his cigarette from his bedroom window onto the porch roof. Then he took his afternoon nap. While he was sleeping the cigarette set the roof on fire. Abram saw it first and called Jacob and others who were Sunday guests. They wakened Jonathan, went through his bedroom with buckets of water, and extinguished the fire. Jonathan's remorse was acute. He never smoked cigarettes in the house after that.

Abram wanted to be like his brother Jonathan. We both copied his manners. His cigarettes were appealing, especially to Abram. He managed to get a few. Then we took long walks on Sunday afternoons to Pool Forge and crept around some of the old buildings there while we smoked the

84

cigarettes. Smoking didn't bother Abram, but it made me sick and dizzy.

"Jonathan got used to them. We can too," Abram encouraged.

"I'm not going to try it. They make me too sick."

"Your Pop smokes and chews."

"I know he does. He gets sick if he quits," I admitted.

Abram wanted to use my bicycle one Sunday afternoon to visit some of his friends who lived near Blue Ball.

"I'll give you this pack of cigarettes, if you let me use your bike this afternoon."

"They make me sick."

"You must try longer, more often."

"Use the bike and keep the cigarettes."

"You give up too easy."

"Well, I'll try again."

I accepted Abram's offer and spent the afternoon alone with a few of those cigarettes. At the extreme west end of Jacob's farm there was a grove of large maple trees. There in shade I tried once more to tolerate smoking. Each cigarette made me sick and dizzy. After the third one I gave it up in anger and disgust.

At evening chore-time Abram came back with my bike. He looked bright and rosy. I was still groggy.

"How did you make out?"

I returned the unused cigarettes.

"You didn't smoke any."

"Three."

"Oh, you've got to try longer than that."

"I don't like them."

"They don't bother me." He stuck the cigarettes in his pocket. "Sorry you don't like them."

"I hate them."

Abram went home. I did the evening chores. When

the work was done, I felt better. The strong smell of the cow stable had smothered out the lingering odor of the cigarettes. The fumes of the cow stable seemed more acceptable.

* * *

"He's dead!"

"No, he's still breathing."

"Take his pulse."

"Yes, he's alive. Hurry, call the doctor."

Someone ran to the neighbor's house to make the phone call.

"What happened?" The neighbors wanted to know.

"The hay-hook got caught in hayloft timbers. When he jerked it loose, it fell down and hit him on the head. He's lying on the barn floor. Jacob thought he was dead, but he's still breathing. Tell the doctor to hurry."

The neighbors came running to the barn where Rebecca's father was lying on the floor. They offered to help.

"Should we carry him to the house?"

"Wouldn't it be better to have him rest here on the soft hay until the doctor comes?"

"Is he bleeding?"

"No, it just hit him on the head and knocked him off the wagon."

"Yes, he's bleeding a little from his nose and ears."

"Get a bucket of warm water and washrags."

"Bring a pillow for his head and a blanket."

The doctor examined Rebecca's father very carefully.

"Other than a severe concussion of the brain, I can find no injuries. There may be a fracture in the skull, but to make sure about that, you would have to take him to the hospital."

Rebecca's father was carried to the house.

Haymaking stopped for that day. I unhitched the horses from the haylift and put them in the stalls.

The tobacco patch always provided work. There was hoeing, weeding, worming to be done endlessly. Later the big stalks, as they approached maturity, had to be topped and suckered. Each was a tedious task. Worming was the job to which I was assigned most frequently. Tobacco worms were always a great threat from planting to harvesting of the crop.

"You'll hunt tobacco worms this afternoon," Jacob said. "I'll take Rebecca and the children to town to do some shopping. On the way home, we'll visit Grandpa Martin."

That meant a long afternoon in the tobacco patch alone. It was a messy job, but the worms were spoilers. They grew as thick as a big man's thumb and twice as long and were able to devour the best leaves in a short time.

The big, horny worms could be handled in any way you desired: pick them from the leaves, throw them on the ground, and smash them with a stick; or fill a tin can and smash them with stones; or throw them on the ground with enough force to burst them wide open; or step on them with your bare feet until the green slimy juice came up between your toes. No matter which way you did it, the operation was not a very delightful one.

Jacob used Beechnut Chewing Tobacco. He seemed to like it. Why shouldn't I? That morning he had opened a new pack and laid it on the shelf beside the watering trough. That would take away the gruesome boredom of my assignment.

My enjoyment was short lived!

The taste was good.

It was fun to spit out the juice like Jacob did.

But in a few minutes it sickened me. Everything within range of my vision turned upside-down. All was going around like a crazy merry-go-round. I fell on the ground under the big tobacco leaves, fearing that I had been poisoned to death. When I recovered, I got after those worms in an angry mood, hating them and the cursed stuff they ate.

At the age of five I had spent a large part of the summer in Jacob's home. When I was eight, I spent most of the summer with him. There I learned much that I had not learned at home. Much of what the boys of the community shared was untrustworthy, data that had to be unlearned later. Still, some of their knowledge was authentic. When Jacob's second child, a son, was born, I shared the news.

"Last night the doctor brought a baby boy to Jacob and Rebecca."

"The doctor didn't bring the baby."

"Yes, he did."

"Jacob said so?" they asked.

"Well, he lied to you. Rebecca gave birth to the baby."

I insisted that the doctor brought the baby and gave it to Jacob and Rebecca.

"You're dumb."

They all laughed at me.

The oldest boy said, "Rebecca carried the baby in her body in the same way the cows, dogs, and cats do." He laughed and added, "You really are dumb!"

I refused to believe a word of it.

"You've seen cows give birth to calves, haven't you?" He questioned me, still laughing. "Or pigs?"

"Yes, I saw the sow giving birth to little pigs, but they are animals. We are people, and that makes a big difference."

"People are just like animals!"

And then he explained the whole process from beginning to end in great detail.

Later I asked Jacob about it.

"Sure," he replied and walked away.

The matter was perplexing!

Why did they make me believe that the doctor brought the babies? Had they told me a lie? In school at Christmas time, Pop refused to permit me to participate in the program because a Santa Claus was to be there to give presents to the pupils. He said the Santa Claus story was a lie. It was a sin to tell a lie. Santa Claus made children believe in a lie. Therefore, Santa Claus was a sin.

To the boy's explanation about the birth of human babies Jacob had said, "Sure," and then he hurried away.

The truth began to come through to me slowly. Perhaps sometimes it is easier to tell a lie than to explain the truth.

\* \* \*

The summer with Jacob at Pool Forge came to an end. Back on my father's farm the land was becoming as dear to me as the mill had been. Through the years with Jacob and on Pop's farm, work in the open air under summer and winter skies, in sun and cloud, heat and cold, calm and storm, was growing increasingly meaningful. Each evening something akin to ecstasy swept through my being as I viewed Sheep Hill Mountain from our yard fence. In the cool, stillness of the evening the Whip-poor-will sang, the turtle dove cooed, and the trilling notes of the warbling robin filled the air. When the barn was filled with new hay, the wheat stood in shocks over the hillside, and the cows grazed contentedly in the meadow near the spring by the old oak tree, gratitude for life brought the day to a peaceful close.

The variety of animal coition that one observed daily on the farm became a pressing curiosity. Cows, pigs, sheep, horses, and even chickens were mated with the greatest of care. All attention was focused on the birth process. Offspring was not to be lost. This phase of life on the farm turned out to produce the greatest crisis in my youthful days.

Pop's best cow was giving birth to her calf, but the delivery did not go well. He placed an urgent call for the veterinarian. It was Monday morning, and the doctor was very slow in coming. Pop was becoming increasingly worried, impatient, and even angry. In a loud voice he ordered me to get busy cleaning out the cow stable on the opposite side of the feeding hall. Father stayed with the cow, pacing back and forth in the stable, timing every period of labor, and cursing with German expletives at every failure.

When the veterinarian arrived, we discovered he had been drinking. Instead of attending the cow, he told Pop about his weekend episode with his women. He called them whores. I had read about whores in the Bible. Passages such as Leviticus 19:20; 20:7-9 and Deuteronomy 22:21; 23:17-18 had made it clear to me that such talk and activity were sinful.

Pop's angry voice exposed his inner tension. "I called you to help this cow! Get on with it. I'm afraid she'll die."

"She won't die."

The doctor fumbled in his bag for the proper instrument as he continued to describe his weekend activities.

"Get busy!" Pop shouted at him. "Do something; help the cow; she's my best one."

The doctor proceeded. Minutes later the calf lay on the straw behind its mother.

Pop swore in German. The doctor swore in English. "I expected as much," he said, slurring the words over his thick tongue.

The calf was dead!

"You drunken louse," Pop shouted.

"Calf was dead long before you called me. I could not have done a thing to save it." He looked at Pop through his bloodshot eyes. "Don't be so mad." He swore emphatically then talked more about his whores.

They pulled the dead calf back against the wall. But the

cow bellowed for it. So they dragged it up to her head and let her clean it with her tongue. At least it silenced the animal.

The doctor's talk grew more vivid.

Pop's anger went out of bounds. He grabbed the doctor by the shoulders and shook him. *"Aus,"* he shouted. *"du mit hund geschlectlichkeit machen!"*

"Take the calf out into the cornfield and bury it deep," Pop said when the doctor had gone.

"Sure."

"But finish the stables first."

"Yes." I cleaned the stalls, filled them with fresh straw for the next milking, and mourned with the grief-stricken cow as she cleaned and loved her dead calf. My thoughts, though, were on that last phrase which my father had shouted in the doctors face. I pulled the dead calf away from its mother's face. She bellowed and pulled at the chain which held her in her stall. On my way back from the cornfield I wondered whether Pop really meant what he had said. My thoughts inevitably involved my own beautiful, loving, female collie dog.

Collie was a very affectionate dog. She was obedient, intelligent, and gentle—golden all over except for the white collar around her neck and her white paws. She brought the cows from the field at milking time. She warned strangers firmly that she was the guardian of our farm. She announced any disturbance at night with a vigor that demanded attention, and yet she was playful with all who offered no threat to our farm or family. Still, she had one fatal flaw!

She ate raw eggs.

Pop wanted her to be shot, but I had pleaded to save her. He gave in to my pleas as we tried many ways to keep her from destroying eggs. Pop gave her severe scoldings and whippings. He tied her in the pig stable attic for weeks at a time. We fed her with different kinds of special food preparations recommended by the veterinarian. As a last effort, we put heavy doses of red pepper in eggs and laid them out for her. She ate them and nearly went wild with the burning red pepper in her mouth, but nothing cured her addiction.

"We've got to shoot her," Pop said.

"Let's try one more time," I begged earnestly.

"You'll keep her tied?"

"Yes."

"Not one more egg or she's finished." Pop shook his finger at me.

I built a house for Collie and kept her tied down by the orchard fence near the pump house where the tall, green grass waved in the wind. I cleaned and fed her every day and took her for long walks on Sheep Hill Mountain every Sunday afternoon. There on the highest stone of my mountain shrine, we communed with one another and with the love that I felt sure came from the heart of the universe. From that highest stone the valley stretched out before us: from Cedar Lane to New Holland, from East Earl to Terre Hill, from the heart of the mountain range to the Weaverland Mennonite Cemetery where the gravestones sparkled in the sunlight and my grandma lay at peace in her grave. There on that highest stone I felt the first stirrings of maturity, the first urgings to decide for myself what I should do with my life and be as a person. There I felt the first awesome presence of God in my life. Collie and I would return from those hikes in loving, subdued companionship. She seemed to sense the Divine Presence too. We returned to the farm in the valley with our thoughts and feelings washed in love and freedom.

But one autumn day, after all the stable work was done and Collie's kennel was fresh and clean with new straw, I made a deadly mistake. Romping with Collie in the tall grass, my father's phrase, as though satanically inspired, flashed into my mind: "*Aus, du mit hund geschlectlichkeit machen!*" And when Collie, in her wild delirium of affection rolled over on her back and spread herself out before me, I stooped to look.

"So that's what's been going on?"

Pop was standing at the chicken-house door, watching me.

I was frightened out of my senses and cried as I tried to explain. But he would not listen.

"Right now she's got to go. No more of that will be tolerated around here."

"Pop, please, I'll never look again."

"She's got to go!"

"You'll shoot her?"

"No, you will. You brought it all on yourself. It's your own fault. Such behavior!"

I was frozen to the spot, speechless and motionless.

"Take her down to the corner of the orchard by the wagon lane. Chain her to the post, down close to the ground, I'll get the gun and the shovel. You'll shoot her and bury her."

Weak to the point of collapsing, I followed his orders. In a few moments he arrived with the gun and the shovel. He had brought his new double-barrelled shot-gun, which he had purchased for the coming hunting season. At different times I had begged him to teach me how to use it, but he never allowed me to touch it.

"Now you'll have a chance to use my new gun."

At the moment I thought it was the most cruel thing he could have said. I almost hated him as I took the highly polished weapon from his hand.

"Both chambers are loaded, but I'm sure you'll need only one. You've got her well tied. Use the first trigger and shoot her right between the eyes. That'll be short and quick."

I held the muzzle of the big gun close to Collie's head, right between her eyes. But her eyes were so full of love, kindness, and trust—even now she was wagging her tail in loving confidence—that I was unable to pull the trigger.

"Shoot!" Pop yelled angrily. "Shoot!"

I stepped to the side and shot her below the left ear. Blood gushed out. Collie moved her head far enough to look into my eyes. In frenzied anquish I instantly aimed the gun between her eyes and pulled the second trigger. The blast blew her brains out and splattered them on the ground at my feet.

"There, now." I gave the gleaming gun to Pop.

"Bury her in the upper corner of the orchard." He walked back toward the house. At the back kitchen door he turned and shouted, "When you've got her buried, come on in for supper."

"Supper," I whispered and stooped to remove the chain from the post. Then I dragged her body to the spot where Pop wanted her buried.

I laid her body, with its mangled head and bloody throat, into the grave upon the bed of clean, new straw which I had just placed in her kennel. When the burial was completed, I threw the shovel upon the ground and sat down on top of Collie's grave. There I buried my face in my knees and cried.

Late at night my ears still rang with Pop's accusation. It rolled over and over and seemed like thunder in my ears: "It's all your fault. Such behavior!"

Mom called from the back kitchen door and came out to my side. "Look," she said, "it's not only you Pop was angry about. He was troubled all day long over another matter. He just blew up when he saw you playing with Collie in the grass."

"What was he so upset about?"

Mom didn't answer.

94

"Then it wasn't just my fault?"

"No."

"If Pop lost his temper about something else, it was his fault too that Collie had to be killed."

"You did what Pop told you to do. Come in. Get some sleep. I'll leave the back kitchen door open for you."

Mom's form disappeared into the dark.

My thoughts turned to the problem that Pop was facing. I wondered about his difficulties. In bed I fell asleep thinking about him, wondering about his worries. But the scene of that awful night did not vanish from my mind. Dreams and wakful memories of the sound of Pop's shot-gun startled me again and again. The sight of Collie's tender, loving eyes shot to shreds kept me in a constant state of remorse.

One evening, while I was splitting wood for the cookstove and stacking it in the woodshed behind the house, Pop came to me and motioned for me to sit on a log by his side.

"It was my fault, not yours," he said. "I did wrong."

I looked at him in silence.

"I'm sorry," he said. "Can you forgive me?"

"Sure, I have already forgiven you, but may I tell you now what I wanted to explain that night and you were too angry to listen?"

"Sure." He seemed surprised.

"Do you remember what the doctor talked about?"

Pop frowned and bowed his head.

"His whores."

"Yes, I guess he did." Pop changed his position.

"The calf was dead; the doctor talked more about his drunken weekend with the women; you were angry and shook him and said, 'Get out! You would commit adultery with a dog.' When I stooped to look at Collie, I was thinking about what you had said to the doctor."

Pop's face turned white.

A long silence ensued.

"Can you forgive me?"

"Yes, easy, Collie was just a dog. You're my Pop, and I love you and need your love more than anything else in the whole world."

Pop wiped away his tears and drew me to his side.

## A Living Flame

"How much am I offered?" the auctioneer cried in a loud and strident voice. "Who'll bid a hundred dollars?" A hundred? Make it a hundred?"

The man at the side of the ring cracked the whip again.

Pop leaned over to me and whispered into my ear, "The little sorrel won't like that." Before the sentence was completed, the horse jumped, reared, pawed the air, and wheeled, swinging the man at the end of the halter rope from side to side.

An afternoon at the New Holland Sales Barn was always exciting. We had looked over all the horses before the sale began. Pop had chosen the little sorrel.

"He'll be a nice one for you to ride," he had said.

"He is beautiful," I agreed.

Pop had examined and measured him from head to hoof.

In the ring the horse was still balking. The man at the side dropped his whip and grabbed the halter rope, but the animal swung both men off their feet and backed out of the ring toward his stall.

"The horse is only scared. Seventy-five, seventy-five, bid seventy-five."

Dealers drew on their big cigars. Farmers spat tobacco juice on the sawdust. The auctioneer continued to plead for a bid.

"Fifty, fifty, who'll start the bidding at fifty? Think of it," he coaxed, "here's a fine saddle horse for fifty dollars. It's a shame."

In the corridor the men were still struggling with the horse. They were unable to bring him back into the sales ring.

Pop looked at the auctioneer and raised his hand.

"Fifty I got. Now we're on the way. Who'll make it sixty?" He shouted, auctioneered, and coaxed in high style. "Going, going, gone for fifty dollars to Sammy Gehman."

Pop paid the cashier. Then we went to the stalls. He spoke quietly to the little Morgan he had just purchased, brushed his flame-like reddish mane, and slipped a bridle over his ears. On our way from the sales grounds, we drove by truck loads of chickens, ducks, geese, corrals of cows and steers, wagon loads of hay and straw, and rows of farm machinery. The horse followed quietly behind our buggy.

"What shall we name him?" Pop asked.

"Let's call him Flame."

"Flame?" Pop studied. "Yeah, that's a good name for him. His tail and mane, and even the color over his body, are reddish like a flame. That'll suit him all over."

\* \* \*

On a cold autumn day a strange wagon appeared in our barnyard drive. It looked like a Mennonite carriage; but it was much bigger and gray instead of black. From the stable I saw the stranger tie his horse to our yard gate hitching post. He was a handsome, clean-cut man and his small, well-shaped beard added distinction to his appearance. His stride was straight, strong, and vigorous.

At mealtime I entered the kitchen by way of the back door. Mom and my sisters were working at the table. Eli and Edwin were sitting behind the stove on the old family settee. Harvey and Paul were in the washroom. Pop and the stranger were already engaged in a lively conversation. The stranger spoke our German language fluently. They were happy over the fact that their first names were the same.

The handsome visitor was Sammy Rubenstein—a Jewish peddler who sold dry goods materials and work clothes. Sammy Rubenstein explained to us that he was a Russian Jew who had come through the war and the 1917 Revolution. Later he came to the United States with his family and now was trying to make a living as a country peddler. In this very modest manner he asked my parents to allow him to show them what he was selling. Pop was so deeply impressed by the story that he immediately urged the salesman to unhitch his horse for noon feeding and himself have dinner with us.

At the dinner table Sammy Rubenstein described vividly the violence and disorder that prevailed during the Russian Revolution. Property rights were wiped away and great confusion followed. Everything was understood to be for everybody's use. No one could count anything as his own. All things were proclaimed as belonging to all people. If you tied your team to a railing in front of a town store, or any other place, you could expect that some other person had it in use by the time you returned from your business in the store.

The peddler kept us spellbound for a long time as he delineated the details of that wild and strange experience during the great transition. But then in a kind and thoughtful manner he turned his attention to our farm and our family.

"You have a nice farm here. Are all your children here?"

"Oh, no," Pop explained, "this group is only the younger half of our family. The others are married and in their own homes."

"Tell me about them."

"Henry, the oldest one, is a pattern-maker for the New Holland Machine Company. He lives in New Holland. Jacob, our second son, lives on a farm at Pool Forge. Samuel, the third, is in the automobile repair business here in East Earl. Noah, the fourth, is farming near Blue Ball, and Isaac, the fifth, is on a farm near New Holland. Two of our boys are dead."

"In the war?"

"No, they died very young."

"Oh, you are Mennonites. You don't take up arms."

"We are conscientious objectors to war."

"Yes, yes, I know. War is surely wrong."

"The rest here can tell you their own names."

"Please." Sammy Rubenstein began with the youngest one.

"I'm Paul."

"Harvey."

"Clayton."

"Katie."

"Susie."

"Eli."

"Edwin."

"And this is Liddy," Pop said, "the gracious little woman who gave birth to all these children."

"Wonderful," Sammy Rubenstein said. Then he continued, looking straight at me. "That third boy. His name again, please."

My heart raced. My thoughts went into a whirl. I gulped, swallowed, and felt myself turning pale and weak.

"Your name, please?"

"Clayton." My voice was pinched tight. Why should he point me out from all the rest? Could his clear eyes see what had happened to Collie and me. The sound of the gun, the sight of Collie's mangled head and throat, the playful

100

CHILDREN OF THE CONESTOGA

ecstasy in the tall orchard grass, and Pop's shout from the chicken-house door swept through my memory.

"Thank you, Clayton," he said. Then he turned to Pop. "Is he going to high school? Will you send him to college? Maybe to law school or medical school?"

"Oh, no," Pop answered firmly. "We Mennonites do not believe in higher education. It leads to pride and loss of faith in our simple way of life. Our children stay at home and work on the farm as soon as the law allows."

"Well, we Jews are like you Mennonites in many ways. We want to protect and keep our faith for ourselves and our children. You're wise to do the same."

The conversation turned to other topics. My thoughts did not follow. Sammy Rubenstein displayed his goods after dinner. Mom and Pop bought many things from him and urged him to be sure to stop in the next time. When the deal was over he reloaded his carriage and went on his way.

Flame loved the wooded trails on Sheep Hill Mountain as well as I did. He pushed his way through the under growth and climbed the steep banks and rocks with sure-footed strength. At the top, where Collie and I had built our mountain altar, he climbed with me and stood by my side on the highest stone.

The valley below was resting sleepily in the gray autumn stillness. The leaves had gone from the trees. The fields were brown and bare. Here and there herds of cattle were milling around in groups, grazing on the frosty grass. The corn was in the barns and the fodder stood on large shocks. The meadow lands lay silent in the hollows. It seemed as though the Creator once more was brooding over the mountain and the valley below, moving onward in his Eternal Purpose.

Sammy Rubenstein had awakened within me a wild, consuming desire to face the future in accordance with my own ambitions. If I should plan to break away from Pop's restraints and go to school some day in the future, would he be disappointed bitterly? Would Mom and Pop say that I turned my back upon their goodness and love? Would they still love me? Would I have the courage to go against their wishes and beliefs?

Flame nuzzled my shoulder and pushed his warm nose against my cheek. He pawed impatiently. I responded to his wishes and took him from that rocky rendezvous with God. Some other day we would come back and feel again the power of the Spirit who awakens restless longings to grow, achieve, and serve humankind in the framework of eternal values.

\* \* \*

"This man needs a good whipping," Edwin shouted to Pop. "Stop all the machinery. He's going to get it now!"

Pop was standing at the granary door. Our late autumn threshing was in full progress. All the men were at work, pitching sheaves from the mow, feeding them into the threshing machine, carrying the grain into the bins, and stacking the straw in the barnyard.

"We're going to settle this fight right now!" With clenched fists Edwin approached his rival on the straw-stack.

"Not here," the man said, "if I should hurt you here on your property, you would have me arrested."

"On the road, if that suits you better." Edwin pointed down over the stack toward the road.

Edwin and I and a third man who traveled with the threshing gang were building the strawstack. The rig man was supposed to push the straw to Edwin in well-formed heaps to facilitate the building of a strong stack. But to irritate Edwin, he pushed it in wide, scattering movements, making the job of building the stack impossible.

102

CHILDREN OF THE CONESTOGA

"You dumb Dutchman," the man said to Edwin, "you talk big. Why, I could push your face out through the back of your head with my little finger."

All the machinery had come to a dead standstill, and the men in the barn had gathered at the doors and windows to see what was going on out on the stack.

"Get him, Edwin," one shouted. "He needs it."

"Sock it to him."

"He's been itching for a good licking a long time."

"Easy, Edwin," Pop advised.

"Did somebody get hurt?" The engineer had just come upon the scene from his place at the controls of the big steam engine on the barn-bridge. "Why did we shut down?"

"Not yet, but soon," somebody shouted.

The rig man looked at his gangmates. "This fellow, this Dutchman? Huh? I can knock him off this stack with my elbow."

I took refuge under the conveyor.

Edwin pushed his tormentor against the conveyor shaft and choked him until his face was blue and his tongue hung out.

"Come on, Chuck, get him," a voice from the gang urged. "Stand up to that Mennonite pacifist. Show him how to fight."

"Stop it," Pop ordered from the granary window.

Two men jumped from the barn upon the stack and restrained Edwin.

The gang foreman confronted Chuck. He swore generously, threatening to fire Chuck.

"You've been asking for this a long time. Either you do your work right or leave the gang." The foreman prepared to give Chuck his severance pay. "Which shall it be?"

Chuck shifted his chewing tobacco from one side of his mouth to the other. "I'll work."

The men went back to their places. In moments all the machinery was running again, and we were building the stack quietly and in order.

## Born Again

"Who wants to go to the big meeting tonight?" Eli asked at the supper table as he explained that our Cousin Amos Horst was conducting evangelistic services at the New Weaverland Mennonite Church.

"Phares and I are going," Susie said. Phares Martin was her boy friend.

"I want to go," Katie said.

"I'd like to go too," I looked at Pop, hoping he would give me his consent.

"U—uh, I think you'd better not. You go with us to the old church for a while yet." He looked at me sympathetically.

"But Cousin Amos is preaching." I knew that approach would touch a warm spot in Mom's thoughts. Cousin Amos was her brother Reuben's son, and he was a famous and powerful preacher in the New Weaverland Mennonite Church.

"Well, let me think about it until the evening chores are done." Pop and Mom exchanged glances. In her eyes it seemed as though Mom was saying that it would be all right for me to go.

That night the climax of maturing youthfulness came upon me. My mother's faith in *Der Gut Mann* had always been a great force in my life, even from the days of my earliest recollections. But that evening, listening to Cousin Amos, the Spirit of the Lord came upon me in a way that I had never felt before. It was a gripping, sweeping, lifting force, and I stood, with others, in confession that Jesus Christ is Lord and Savior. Details of the evening have vanished, but the overwhelming joy of that moment, the glorious sense of Divine Being, the maturing, cleansing, empowering unity with the Eternal has remained. The reality of having been made into a "new creature in Christ" endures.

That new commitment was put to an unexpected test before many months had passed by. Isaac's wife, Catherine, became helplessly and painfully ill with inflammatory rheumatism. Help was requested in caring for her, the four children, and the work in the barn. One evening he explained the situation to Mom and Pop.

Should Susie or Katie go and help with the work at the house? Should one of the boys take care of all the chores at the barn? Isaac concluded that the most helpful approach to his needs would be for some one to do the farm chores, thus setting him free to nurse his wife and take care of the children. The final decision named me as the one to assume responsibility for all farm chores. It was a challenging assignment.

I started for his home, south of New Holland, on a cold, early winter night. Flame puffed out his breath in little, white clouds; the frost bit at my nostrils; and the frozen snow reflected the glare of the setting sun.

"Put your horse in the stable," Isaac called from the kitchen door, "and come in for supper. You can do the chores afterward."

The children were sitting at the table, patiently waiting. Catherine was screaming in pain in her bedroom next to the kitchen. Isaac had gone to comfort her. Four sober faces looked at me, then smiles formed. The children asked about Flame and the cold ride from East Earl to New Holland.

Earl, the oldest of the four children, started the conversation and the others followed. It seemed as though it was more difficult for me than for them to be composed in the presence of their mother's cries of pain.

"Did you mind the cold?" Earl was obviously trying to help me feel at home. "Did your new horse behave well?"

"Yeah, he's very calm."

"Was he afraid of the cars?" Benjamin, the second of the family, wanted to know. "Did he balk?"

"No." I found it almost impossible to wrest my thoughts away from the sickroom. "No, no, oh, no. He's not a bit balky, if I'm kind to him and talk quietly. He depends upon me."

Mildred and Grace, the next in order of age, sat silently at the table, listening to their father speaking comfortingly to their mother.

"When you don't want him any more, will you give him to me?" Benjamin asked.

"Would you take good care of him and be kind to him?"

"The very best," he promised.

"I'll keep that in mind."

Isaac returned to the table. Following his prayer of blessing, we ate our meal in happiness as the children shared excitement over the Christmas program which was being planned at their school. The school building stood across the street and a few hundred feet down the road.

The food on the table was cooked corn-mush, potatoes, green beans, fried ham, bread, butter, jelly, peanut butter, crackers, and a large pitcher of milk. While we were eating, Isaac gave me instructions concerning the chores: ten cows were waiting to be milked by hand; fifteen steers to be run to the watering trough and fed; five horses, ten pigs, and two hundred chickens waiting for similar evening care. The milk was to be properly cooled and the eggs gathered and carried to the house basement where they were to be graded and crated for market.

Silage, hay, corn fodder, and all the other feed was to be put in proper place for the 5:00 a.m. feeding. In the morning, the same routine was to be carried out in time to get the milk to the New Holland railroad station by seven o'clock. Time between morning and evening chores was spent in the tobacco stripping room. Some good neighbors were helping with the work in the tobacco cellar.

Catherine's sickness, in spite of the best care the family physician could give, ran its course. My bedroom was upstairs in a room which was located directly above hers. Isaac slept on a small couch in her room and responded to her calls many times each night. Her cries awakened me frequently. Each night her calls struck deeper into my sensitivities. I prayed, wondered, and questioned. Often I fell asleep instantly. Then hour by hour, I was startled wide awake as Catherine's screams shivered through the house. Each morning, at four-thirty, Isaac called me to get started with the morning chores. The unavoidable Philadelphia milk train arrived at New Holland at seven o'clock each day. It was a stern deadline that knew no mercy and offered no grace.

The children's school Christmas program offered a happy diversion. Neighbors came to stay with Catherine so that Isaac and I could enjoy and participate in the festivities with the children. That program provided exciting table conversation for a long time, both before and after Christmas. It created an island of happiness in a sea of misery.

Heavy snows began to fall late in December and kept the roads impassable most of the time through January and February. Farmers opened fences and found ways through the fields with their wagons and sleighs. Strong winds frequently swept away the tracks. The deep drifts or snow were reshifted constantly. Many mornings the trip to the New Holland milk station was a trial and error battle with high winds and blowing snow. Those pre-dawn exposures to the blasts of winter's merciless cold intensified my awareness of the cruelties in nature's mighty power.

The end of January found me in a weary and exhausted condition. Sympathy, patience, and physical energy were spent. My simple faith in an all-wise, all-loving, and all-powerful Creator was being shaken. "Why does God allow this terrible, savage suffering?" The question tortured me day after day as I went about the chores in rain, sleet, snow, and blinding blizzard. Bitterness and despair loomed large.

Isaac's prayers at the table and family worship implored God to give us patience, courage, and strength to endure the ordeal. At the time I marveled at his warmth of faith and love. Later I learned that Isaac and Catherine, in a love nest all their own near the banks of the Conestoga Creek on a balmy, summer evening, pledged their lives to one another at the early age of middle adolescence. Then I understood! Still, in the face of the next day's endless work and weariness, I encountered further doubts. Maybe, after all, the view of *Der Gut Mann* to which my mother adhered so passionately was unrealistic. Wonderful, if true! But how could one know? Sometimes those questions grew to painful and tormenting proportions. My feelings hardened, at times, to the point of saying, "The hell with it all!"

In the barn, I was a loner. The animals provided some companionship. They trusted my presence and greeted me morning and evening with eager anticipation. The fierce winter lashed and whipped at the corners of the building, but the barn, filled with hay, straw, shredded corn-fodder, and tons of bags of feed, provided a mighty fortress against its deadly blasts. Week after week, the trip to the mill with a load of corn on the bobsled was an absolute necessity.

While the miller was grinding the grain, I warmed myself by the fire in his office heater and studied the colorful packages of chewing tobacco, cigarettes, cigars, pipes, and pipe tobacco. *Prince Albert*! What a beautiful name! And the package? The bright red tin can! How attractive! "Could I smoke a pipe?" The question teased me. It might be different from chewing tobacco and smoking cigarettes. In my effort to be tough, to avoid breaking down in the midst of my battle with sickness, cold, weariness, and loneliness, I bought a pipe and a can of Prince Albert. On my way home, I blew out clouds of smoke into the icy wind and swore that my father was an inconsiderate heel for letting me struggle alone in this intolerable situation. But before I got to Isaac's barn, I threw the fancy pipe and the shiny box of Prince Albert into a big snow bank along the way.

But the ordeal came to an end. Catherine regained her health. The winter relaxed it's severity. Concerning that trial, I remember most vividly the tenacious, unyielding love and tenderness with which Isaac cared for his wife. I had learned that God's glory can be felt in suffering, toil, and severe exposure as well as in surroundings of beauty and peace. I had learned that love is God's creative power at work where people need each other.

## The Dispersion

Change, drastic change, had come into our family. Pop had bought an automobile! He learned to drive it. It was a little, four-cylinder Overland, a "puddle jumper." The Old Order Bishops had decided to permit the use of motorcars by members of the church. But there were limitations. They allowed touring cars, not sedans. Everything had to be in black, not nickle-plated. Even the door handles and the bumpers had to be painted black. The Black Bumper Mennonites had made their appearance in the Weaverland area.

More change came. Edwin and Susie married and moved away from home. Eli bought a truck and went into business for himself, hauling milk for the East Earl Creamery. Katie got work in a Lancaster hospital as a cook. Mom and Pop retired. They moved to a house in the village near Samuel's garage. Jacob moved from Pool Forge to the home farm at East Earl. Paul stayed at home with Mom and Pop. Harvey and I worked on our brothers' farms for a few short years. Then we faced the open market to find our jobs and make our way in the world.

Little by little we were lured away from the enchanting powers of the Conestoga Valley. But during the days of transition we still spent many happy hours there.

Nothing was more exciting after a hard day's work on the

111

farm than to go for a swim in the Conestoga. The big dam near the Weaverland Mennonite Churches was the favorite swimming hole in the community.

"I'll bet I can swing out farther and higher on this rope than you can." That was a common challenge that rang through the air on a hot summer evening on the high bank at the big dam.

"Prove it."

"Who'll be the judge?"

"Pete. He doesn't swim anyway."

A diving board and a rope tied to the highest branch of a large overhanging tree provided the equipment for the water sports of the group.

My turn came.

"Give it all you got," Edwin said, as I grasped the rope.

I responded to his word of encouragement. It meant a lot to me. He had an important job as a carpenter. Maybe some day I'd have a job working with him. I put all my strength into the action and went far and high out over the waters of the Conestoga, pulling myself upward on the rope to gain additional elevation. Then I dropped, twisted, and dived down toward the water.

"Look out!" The fellows on the bank were shouting and waving their arms in great excitement.

With an awful, crackling, splintering sound the tree broke off at the root and came falling down upon me. The group on the bank stared in helplessness. I sank beneath the surface. Down, down, down to the bottom I went and swam along the sandy, muddy creek floor. The giant tree with its wide-spreading branches would kill me outright or pin me to the soft bosom of the Conestoga and never let me go. It was the end of me. My thoughts swam with me. Nothing could save me. The fellows on the bank were horrified and helpless. They could only stand and watch. That I knew!

112

The Conestoga, the lovely Conestoga, the source of all my joys, the pride of my life, the place I never wanted to leave, now was smothering me in its loving and cruel, unrelenting embrace. I must breathe!

The branches of the big tree settled to the bottom and pressed on my shoulders, my head, my back, my legs. I must breathe! I struggled and got free. Upward! I brushed and struggled through the intricate network of branches. Air! Breath! I had to hold or die. That I knew. Upward, upward. The big branches seemed to hold me, lift me. Things darkened. My lungs exploded. I was gone. The Conestoga had claimed me!

When I regained consciousness, I was clinging to the big branches, and my nose had risen just above the water. Air! Light! I was not dead! The tree, with its mighty arms, held me up. I saw the men, including Edwin, standing stunned on the bank. I was dazed and weak, not sure that what I felt and saw was real. Edwin and several other men made their way over the fallen tree and assisted me to shore.

Murmuring broke out in the amazed group as other persons arrived for their evening swim.

"What happened?"

"My gosh!"

"He's alive!"

"Thank God!"

"Is he hurt?"

"Doesn't seem like it."

"Better take him to a doctor."

"The whole tree!"

"It's all down, clean from the roots."

Edwin took me to Doctor John Winters' office and explained what had happened.

The doctor went over me carefully. "You're not hurt," he assured me. "Your guardian angel must have been with you. That's all I can say."

"I never expected him to get out of that situation alive," Edwin said, "and he's not even hurt."

"It's a miracle. It really is," the doctor said, shaking his head in amazement.

"It was a miracle." The doctor's words stuck in my thoughts and did not go away. He went over me again, and then, with a tremor in his voice, he said, "The Conestoga and the Lord were very kind to you. I hope you will make good use of the life they let you keep."

I swallowed and choked back my emotions.

Edwin remained silent.

"That was a close call," the doctor said, still shaking his head in wonderment. "A close call." He stared at me. "Take care. Make good use of your life. You were either in God's hands or mighty lucky."

## EPILOGUE

Mom and Pop had espoused a very practical, simple, and honest faith in the love and mercy of God—*Der Gut Mann*. Their religion influenced me beyond measure. Mom's life was directed by one great passion, namely, to serve the living Jesus. She impressed that commitment upon me so deeply that I thought of Jesus as an embodied human being still living on this earth. A playmate in the Conestoga schoolyard corrected me one day. He explained that Jesus was Spirit not a human being on earth. I was so shaken by his explanation that I could not get it out of my mind for the rest of the day. In the evening, as soon as I got home from school, I asked Mom about the matter. She answered immediately by saying, "Yes, Jesus is Spirit. We are his human body. He lives in all who love him and keep his commandments. The church is his body."

Pop put his faith to work in his generous attitude toward those who held differing views. He listened with patience, responded kindly, accepted criticism, but always stayed with the Old Weaverland Mennonite Church in whose shadow he was born and reared.

Pop's home was less than a half mile from the church on a road going west. He was born there on the last day of February in the year of 1871. Mom's home was a little farther away from the church on a road going north. She was born there on November 3 in the year of 1873. Pop's only broth-

115

er—he had no sisters—died early in life. Mom grew up in a very large family with many brothers and sisters. That old stone church in Weaverland was the center of their life. From that fellowship they drew their spiritual breath, developed their Christian stature, and maintained their simple and practical faith in *Der Gut Mann*. The simplicity and power of that faith, with its underlying humility, has followed us as "children of the Conestoga" in all our separate lives and ways. Either God had his hands upon us or we were mighty lucky. But as children of the Weaverland Mennonite Churches, we commited our lives to the will and saving grace of *Der Gut Mann*, in that sense our lives were and are *in his hands*. With the blessed Savior, we said, "Into Thy hands I commit my spirit." To trace the journey of our love and faith beyond the days of Pop's and Mom's retirement from the East Earl farm requires a story of its own. Here it is sufficient to say that from the time of that dispersion, we went our separate ways, still never very far from home, ceasing not "to teach and preach Jesus Christ."